The Wealth or Health of Nations

The Wealth or Health of Nations

Transforming Capitalism from Within

Carol Johnston

WIPF & STOCK · Eugene, Oregon

Wipf and Stock Publishers
199 W 8th Ave, Suite 3
Eugene, OR 97401

The Wealth or Health of Nations
Transforming Capitalism from Within
By Johnston, Carol
Copyright©1998 Pilgrim Press
ISBN 13: 978-1-60899-588-2
Publication date 7/21/2010
Previously published by Pilgrim Press, 1998

To the great teachers whose patience was transforming:

Harry Maranian

John B. Spencer

Daniel Day Williams

Andrew S. Katsanis

Jane Dempsey Douglass

John B. Cobb Jr.

Contents

Foreword

John B. Cobb Jr.

MODERN ECONOMIC THEORY arose when it became clear that the industrial revolution made possible the increase of wealth. Economists studied how this happened and the social contexts that supported this growth. Initially they took for granted that society, and especially nations, provided the wider context in which wealth was sought. But they did not resist when society decided to make the pursuit of wealth its primary goal and thus made the economy its primary institution and economists its most important guides to public policy.

In an earlier generation Christians took part in the debate between those who wanted the market to be free from bureaucratic control and those who wanted governments to manage the economy for the sake of all the people. With the collapse of Communism and the decline of socialist theory generally, most Christians have now gone along with the victory of global capitalism. Our only role seems to be the amelioration of the suffering of those who do not succeed in market competition.

In fact, however, the economic issues are far from exhausted by the controversy between capitalism and socialism. Indeed, in terms of the consequences of the usual forms of economic growth for human community and the biosphere, capitalism and socialism are hardly distinguishable. Rather than resolving basic issues about the economy, the victory of capitalism over socialism calls for more intensive study of the dominant form of capitalism and the theory that supports it. But few Christians have brought their convictions and insights to bear on this task.

Carol Johnston is an outstanding exception. She knows that if there are to be theoretical changes in economic thinking, there must be a historical understanding of how the particular doctrines that are now taken for granted came into being. Only as they are relativized through this historical study will it be possible for economists to reconsider options that were earlier rejected but that might today prove highly relevant and beneficial. Accordingly, she provides us with a history of economic theory that focuses on the formation of what are now its basic assumptions about the nature of reality, the goals to be sought, and the role of the theory itself.

Much is at stake. The world is rapidly being transformed by economic forces into a relatively homogeneous global market. The once natural environment is being transformed into an artificial one. The rate of global change is vastly accelerated in comparison with any that has occurred before. All this is justified by a theory that has a number of questionable assumptions, some of which are, at the very least, in marked tension with the traditions of all the major religious communities. Many of the actual consequences follow quite directly from these questionable assumptions. Can it be faithful to acquiesce in these global changes uncritically?

It may be that Johnston has made major errors in her historical account, although I am aware of none. It may be that her values are not shared by most other Christians, although I would find that surprising. But even if this were true, she has without doubt problematized ideas that economics as a "science" takes for granted as the premises of a deductive system. She has done so in a way that makes the issues accessible to the general public.

Many Christians recognize the importance of these issues in the context of ethics. Certainly the economic order involves ethical issues. Indeed, Christians are quick to criticize the injustices that the working of the dominant economic order causes.

Unfortunately, as long as the Christian response is at that level only, the basic system remains unchallenged. We have only the role of protest in terms of principles that are hardly relevant to the actual situation except as sources of complaint. If we are to play a serious role, we must engage at a theoretical level the system of beliefs that now finds expression in dominant global practice.

In short, the task Christians confront is theological, and Johnston has written a theological book. That may not be recognized by those who identify theology as an academic discipline neatly marked off from others and focusing on traditional religious beliefs. Johnston does not discuss Jesus Christ or the Holy Spirit or the doctrine of the Trinity. Nor does she rehearse questions about the nature of sin or justification by faith. But her perspective on the discussion that has formed the now dominant economic theory is a confessedly Christian one.

Any history is highly selective and the selection is guided by particular interests and perspectives. Johnston is rightly explicit about her point of view. But what she sees from her Christian perspective is there to be seen by persons who approach matters in other ways. In this sense, her account, although motivated by Christian convictions, is quite "objective." Others may prefer to place the emphasis in different ways and to highlight different features of economic thinking. But this cannot negate the fact that the features she studies are there to be studied and have played their role in shaping our shared destiny.

This means that this book is a contribution to public theology. It is reflection about the issues that most deeply concern the body politic. The Christian point of view functions, not to limit the audience to Christians, but to share with the whole concerned community what a Christian can contribute to the general discussion.

Preface

CORPORATE RESTRUCTURING, pay inequities, and an emerging class system of the haves and have-nots. What has prompted Western interests to become so focused on wealth at the seeming expense of workers, environments, and even at times consumers?

This book seeks to answer this and other questions by returning to the headwaters of Western economic thinking. In Adam Smith's *An Inquiry into the Nature and Causes of the Wealth of Nations* (1776), growth in the production of goods—any goods—became the goal of capitalism, and the self-interested choice of individuals in the marketplace became its powerful engine. An invisible hand, Smith asserted, would connect self-interest with concern for the preservation of communities and nations.

Since then many economists have sought to reorient or refine this economic theory—for example, John Stuart Mill caused a split in the understanding of justice between those focusing on individual freedoms (now often called *conservatives*) and those who were concerned with social equity (*liberals*). But the invisible hand seems to have evaporated, so that loggers square off against spotted owls and home builders against unearthed Native American artifacts.

I write, then, for morally sensitive persons who rightly suspect that many of our current societal values and assumptions are embedded in economic theory and that the assumptions, unless unearthed and examined, are remarkably difficult to argue against. I attempt to report at each turn what a particular economist contributed and what opportunities were missed as the theory got narrower and narrower until only the decisions of individuals in the market were the center of economics, and wealth became the only reality. I close by offering a proposal for transforming capitalism from a focus on wealth to one of concern for community and national health.

No doubt economists will decry an ethical theologian's venturing into their domain, especially when the theories are far more nuanced than I can describe in the brief compass of a chapter and when the many side conversations going on in secondary literature are hardly given a peek. I am keenly aware of this vulnerability, and I will try to provide a thumbnail sketch of Western economic history in the hopes that other thoughtful persons—including theologians, ethicists, and students—will pick up the issues raised here and will work into the broader literature. I know, for example, that many economists will object to my turning to Peter Drucker as reflecting John Maynard Keynes when other works have done a better job. True, but I hope to reach out to the literature that noneconomists are reading.

No doubt theologians will decry the seeming lack of theology in the text. To them the bulk of this book might seem like an intellectual history, especially when the major Western economists are treated seriatim and when one purpose is to provide a map of the intellectual terrain. My insistence on absolute scarcity is a theological-ethical criticism against economists' circumlocution, which maintains, for example, the irrelevance of the total number of barrels of oil in the biosphere and only focuses on the number available at prices consumers will pay given the current level of technology and the accessibility of currently remaining reserves. My goal is to push the conversation beyond understanding to action.

No doubt historians of thought will decry that my major criticism has in one form or another been stated about a dozen times in the past 150 years, namely, that Western economics is overly deductive and individualistic. My response is that such criticisms need to be made—even repeated—until Western societies crack open their economic theory in order to examine the values and assumptions by which we live, embracing some and changing others. More important, we need to move the critique into constructive proposals for transformation, or we will have another 150 years of deductive and overly individualistic economics—if the planet can bear it that much longer.

Acknowledgments

THIS PROJECT BEGAN when John Cobb told me, "If you want to do something that matters, work on economics." Since I was trained in philosophy and theology, it seemed downright odd, and definitely risky, to attempt a theological reading of economics. But it also seemed like an important thing to do, and so it has turned out to be. I owe a great debt to John Cobb for luring me into this work, and even more for standing by me all the way through it. At the same time, I was helped greatly with economics as a discipline by economists Hans Palmer and Gordon Douglass, whose knowledge of economic history and whose staunch defense of neoclassical economic theory forced me to come up with better arguments, and hopefully saved me from many errors. Any that remain are definitely my own.

A special thank-you goes to Jim Lewis, a colleague who volunteered to take some of my workload so that I could finish the manuscript, and thanks also to Richard Dickinson and Craig Dykstra, who were patient with me as I struggled to fit everything in.

Finally, I want to thank my editor, Timothy Staveteig, and The Pilgrim Press. When other publishers were reluctant to take a risk on an interdisciplinary project that crosses traditional boundaries, he and his colleagues understood the importance of encouraging work that attempts to find fresh thinking for dealing with real social problems. May they be amply rewarded for their courage!

Introduction: The Choices for Wealth over Health of Nations

I F *THEY* could do it, *we* can do it. *They* were Adam Smith, David Hume, and the other Enlightenment thinkers who set out to figure out how to transform the economic and political systems of the eighteenth century. They were frustrated with the way a few elite members of society controlled the economy through monopolistic mercantilism and landed estates, and the polity through limited democracy (and in most of Europe, no democracy at all). They pushed for the expansion of social participation through freer markets and more democratic governments. They read their society as clearly as they could, picked out trends that could further their cause, and gave those trends a boost through their writings. Adam Smith in particular saw that freeing up local markets would advance participation and at the same time enable the economy to grow. Smith spent years closely observing different economic practices, and thought long and hard about what they meant, and could mean. In 1776, when he published his book, *An Inquiry Into the Nature and Causes of the Wealth of Nations,* he could not have foreseen in his wildest dreams how the nascent capitalism that he described would succeed.

Today the capitalism heralded by Adam Smith is advancing triumphantly across the world. Its only true rival, Marxism, is in retreat everywhere after massive failures. The truth is, capitalism is the only economic system ever devised that has succeeded in creating sustained growth in production. Capitalism brilliantly harnesses human energy for the purpose of maximizing profits in the marketplace, and has thereby unleashed unprecedented amounts of creativity in the service of expanding human consumption. Millions of people have benefited greatly from this process.

At the same time, the development of capitalism has been very costly, and some of its worst effects are built into the system. From the very beginning, industrialization has destroyed communities and cultures, and disrupted the natural environment. This has been true of Marxism even more than of capitalism, but it is no longer possible for us to deny that we must face up to the problems generated in capitalism itself. Even enthusiastic defenders such as

Peter Berger and Michael Novak admit that capitalist development constantly disrupts communities and destroys traditional cultures.[1] The gains in availability and cheapness of goods that were once thought to be luxuries, and the ultimate improvement in individual standards of living, are thought to prove that the costs have been worth it. But even if that is true (and I do not think it is), the costs of capitalism are not just part of the early stages of economic development. Even wealthy societies such as the United States are still paying, and paying dearly. The ever mounting array of consumer goods is accompanied by continually disintegrating communities, disrupted ecosystems, and cultures that have been degraded by rampant consumerism. In the United States we see this most starkly in the poor areas of our inner cities, but it is also true of our wealthy suburbs, where broken homes, drug abuse, passive consumption (a la "couch potatoes"), fear, and spiritual emptiness are endemic. And while we have made great progress in mitigating the worst effects of pollution, we still have not learned how to prevent the economy from generating them. Our whole society has been in a condition of crisis management for a long time, and many of us feel as if our daily lives have been taken over and splintered.

If wealthy societies pay dearly for the successes of capitalism, poor communities pay much more, because they bear the cost of its failures. Older members of many poor communities can remember when they were a community—a neighborhood or a village where people did without material things but were rich in culture and mutual help. But even judging by material wealth alone, millions of people have been victims of clumsy economic development that followed the dictates of capitalist ideology but ignored local realities. One pastor from Kenya recalls when his rural parishioners named their children "Abundance," because they always had enough to live on. But economic "experts" came to them and convinced them that they would get rich if they converted from subsistence farming to coffee production. Instead of getting rich, they got into debt, and at the same time all but destroyed the productive capacity of their land. Consequently, they are materially poorer than they were before "development" came to them. They do not name their children "Abundance" any more. This is but one example, but who could claim that the millions of people trapped in the sprawling urban slums of cities all over the world are better off, either culturally or materially, than their ancestors were before they were pushed off the good farmland? This is not to idealize rural poverty, but to acknowledge that there are different kinds of poverty, and traditional subsistence farming communities managed to be healthier, for the most part, than urban slums have been.

I would never claim that capitalism alone is to blame for all of this. But we will see how capitalism contributes to these problems, and insofar as it does, we must grapple with it. Over the past 150 years, there have been two modes of grappling with the problems generated by capitalist development: Marxism and liberal reforms. Marx eloquently advocated revolution, arguing vehemently that nothing less could destroy the monopoly of the capitalist elites and put control into the hands of the masses. Millions of people who felt keenly the injustices of capitalist societies were inspired by Marxism for over a century. Unfortunately, Marx did not offer a genuine alternative to capitalism that could avoid its abuses. To the contrary, he advocated massive industrialization and deliberate disruption of traditional communities, and he knew exactly what it would cost the very masses that he claimed to care about. Consequently, millions of lives were sacrificed to the idealistic dreams of communism. This is terribly ironic, because the main reason the Marxist dream died was its failure to support the dreams of the masses of individuals Marxism claimed to serve.

In any case, violent revolutions tend to fail to change the underlying dynamics that cause them, and they feed a cycle of violence that is very hard to break. What then of the alternative—liberal reforms? This has been the path pursued in much of the West, and it has clearly been much more successful than Marxism. Liberal reformers, concerned about the excesses of capitalism, have followed the suggestion of John Stuart Mill to accept capitalism's productive genius but ameliorate its problems by means of government regulation and redistribution of the wealth generated. (I call this group the social equity liberals.) By this means (and with pressure from the labor movements) child labor was regulated, factory shifts were reduced from as much as fourteen hours to eight, basic safety and health were improved, the minimum wage and Social Security were instituted, and so on. No one would deny that this approach has helped to lift millions of people out of poverty and into the middle class. But this approach has only ameliorated, not addressed, the persistent problems generated by capitalism. Individuals in Western societies live materially better lives, but are still subject to all the ills listed above.

Reform movements have helped but do not go far enough. Revolutionary movements have been too destructive of the very people they intended to help. My suggestion is that we learn how to foster genuine *transformation*. Like Adam Smith and his Enlightenment colleagues, we need to read our current situation honestly, think long and hard about how to make changes that would foster healthier societies, and identify and support promising trends that will help get our societies moving in the right direction. As I noted above, there is much about capitalism that is effective and that we would not want to lose. Part of the genius of capitalism is the way it harnesses self-interested behavior effectively. However, capitalism has taken self-interested behavior to the unhealthy extreme of enshrining individual choice as the greatest and only admissible social good. One of the transformations needed is to reconnect self-interest and the common good, and not blindly assume that we can trust an "invisible hand" to make individual decisions benefit the whole. When we do this we turn capitalism into an ideology, and that is always dangerous, because ideologies of whatever kind command faith in a set system of ideas instead of honesty about actual situations.

To transform capitalism we have to understand it. It is not enough to rail against its failures and agitate for change. Activism without hard and honest thinking cannot be effective in the long run. We need to examine the economic theory that frames capitalism, explore its current economic, social, and cultural effects, be honest about how it is effective and how it generates problems, and ask what possibilities for transformation already exist within the system. We also need to work hard at keeping the achievements while tackling the problems. I do not advocate outright rejection of modern individualism in favor of a romantic return to premodern societies. I hope we can reconnect fully individual and free persons to healthy communities for their greater flourishing. Finally, we need to figure out how to get past the polarized discourse that splits our societies and weakens our efforts to deal with our problems. For example, the right wing champions "family values" while the left wing agitates for social justice. But what if these are different ways of naming the same reality—the disintegration of our communities and the families within them under pressure from economic individualism? And what if the split between individual freedom and social equity has resulted in a truncation of our understanding of justice and a neglect of the broader element of quality participation in the economy and in society? What would happen if we tried to foster a public discourse in which the focus was on grappling with our actual situation rather than trading ideological phrases? A transformative approach will advocate this kind of attempt to convert conflict into constructive conversation.

This is certainly a daunting task, but surely no more difficult than the one Adam Smith and company set for themselves. It will take many people and many decades, but if they could do it, we certainly can. While I don't aspire to be another Adam Smith, as if such a thing were possible, I do hope this book is a modest contribution to a larger effort to transform capitalism from within. This project concentrates on a particular aspect of that effort: developing an understanding of how capitalism got to where it is now by studying the history of the development of economics. Along the way we will examine the value choices and governing assumptions embedded in capitalist theory, and what possibilities for transformation exist within that history. In the last chapter I will build on the possibilities that exist within capitalism's own history and sketch some proposals for new foundations for a transformed economics. But I hope that someday someone will write a book that surpasses Adam Smith's—an inquiry into the nature and causes of the health of nations.

When we set out to understand economics, we immediately encounter a central aspiration of mainstream contemporary economic theory, called neoclassical economics—to be value-free. The ideal is to impose no values in the course of analysis, but to predict the consequences of various choices and so provide some means of control. Values are supposed to be left entirely up to the preferences of individuals. This position is well enunciated in the classic 1917 essay "The Scope and Method of Political Economy" by John Neville Keynes (father of John Maynard Keynes):

> Political economy is . . . a science, not an art or a department of ethical enquiry. It is described as standing neutral between social schemes. It furnishes information as to the probable consequences of given lines of action, but does not itself pass moral judgments.[2]

This attempt to make economics a value-free "science" has made possible an unprecedented clarity of method. It was a long and difficult process of refinement, and it has made an enormous difference in the capacity of societies to gain some control over their economies. Capitalism has proven to be the engine of growth that Adam Smith hoped it would be, and neoclassical theory has lent itself to economic analysis with a power and clarity for shaping economic choices that no other theory has ever shown.

But this quest for clarity and effectiveness has not been achieved without costs, and it has fostered the problems of capitalist economies that we discussed above. Neoclassical theory, because it is focused intensely on the choices of individuals (and individual firms) in the market, and at the macro level on national policy, does not see these problems and cannot function to prevent or correct them without social intervention. Furthermore, because what happens to communities and ecosystems as such is defined out of economics, even economists who are concerned about them find it difficult to include them in their work—even when it is economic forces that are causing the social and environmental problems. Environmental economics is in its infancy, and while economists are beginning to admit that they need to deal with these problems, they have not as yet gone very deep in their attempts. In the meantime, the economy is structured to keep generating its destructive effects right along with its successes.

When economics was being developed, community values seemed secure and nature seemed vast and untamable. The problem was how to make an economy grow so that more people could be fed and clothed and housed, and any growth was a triumph. But today we have achieved nearly continuous economic growth, and the problem is how to balance it with other social needs. The early economists made assumptions and value choices for economics that made sense in their context and that enabled them to succeed in their goals. Consequently, far from being value-free, economic theory and economies today have these assumptions and value choices still embedded in them, and they are contributing to the problems we are having of balancing growth with the common good. We will examine these embedded values and consider some consequences for the theory, for the actual economy, and for the larger society and culture.

Economics has gone through a long process of refinement and emerged as a distinct academic discipline. Assumptions that were originally tentative and dependent on one context have been "purified" into "laws of economics" that are now taken for granted and applied in radically different contexts. By exploring those original contexts, we can see some of both the positive contributions and the problematic consequences of the choices economists made and can also consider promising elements in each one's work that were later neglected. An examination of the work of the most influential economists should uncover the most crucial choices. The following group exemplifies the historical process well: Adam Smith, David Ricardo and Thomas Malthus, John Stuart Mill, Karl Marx, the school of the marginalists (especially Stanley Jevons and Léon Walras) and Alfred Marshall, and, for the twentieth century, John Maynard Keynes and Milton Friedman. By no means were these economists the only important ones, nor did they single-handedly make all the important choices. Society and culture have influenced the economists and the economy, and vice versa. The influences have been mutual, mutually reinforcing, and crucial; these economists were both exemplars and shapers of what was at work in their societies. Admittedly many economists have held dissenting views all along, and many today do not accept many of the views that these economists held. But the dominant theories and the larger culture bear their legacy, so for good and ill we must deal with it.

Four crucial value choices were made early in the development of economics, and these shaped an economy that now succeeds brilliantly at achieving its primary goal: unlimited growth in the production of goods and services for the sake of individual consumption. Adam Smith himself was responsible for the first two: he chose growth in production as the central goal of economics, and the encouragement of individual self-interested behavior as the best means of achieving growth. Smith's individuals were still rooted in social relations, but over time atomistic individualism took over in economics and in the larger society. The *Homo economicus,* or "wealth-maximizer," of John Stuart Mill assumed away all other social considerations, and later the marginalists and Alfred Marshall refined him into the "rational actor" of the market.

Smith also made the third fateful choice of assigning the source of value to labor instead of to land. Although "land" remained in economic theory as one of the factors of production, it effectively dropped out as a factor in its own right while capitalists and Marxists argued over whether capital or labor is more important.[3] Capitalism treats land as just another form of capital, while Marxism treats it as a form of labor. Either way, there is no provision for safeguarding living natural systems as such—even though all economic activity depends on them. Consequently, even though an endlessly growing economy threatens the integrity of ecosystems worldwide, environmental destruction is defined as "external" to economic questions themselves.

The fourth crucial choice was made by David Ricardo and refined by John Stuart Mill. They selected deductive method as the best means of achieving clarity and effectiveness in economics. Given the immense complexity of actual economies, they made some basic assumptions about human beings and how they behave for economics, and found that these assumptions worked well enough. And they were right, but the cost has been adaptability, because the sole use of deductive method obscures changing realities in actual economies and changing understandings of human nature and the natural world. For over two hundred years Enlightenment individualism and Newtonian mechanism have constituted the governing paradigm of economics. But in the twentieth century atomistic individualism was superseded in both anthropology and physics, and a paradigm based on the relations of complex entities in living natural systems emerged. Unfortunately, the reliance of economists on deductive method has made them reluctant to reexamine their own basic assumptions.

Economics, then, needs to use historical-critical methods as well as deductive method; it needs to reexamine its own fundamental assumptions; and it needs to draw on neglected aspects of its own history to transform itself. It seems odd that economists are so reluctant to allow transformation in their own discipline, when they are so ready to celebrate continuous change in capitalist economies. Although economists are working on grappling with challenges to deductive method, the tendency so far has been to withdraw from the more sweeping claims of the method without really changing the deeply embedded values.[4] Economics is not the only discipline that needs to do this. Most of the disciplines have become too narrowly defined and have neglected their own foundations for too long. However, the enormous impact of economics makes its transformation especially urgent.

One of the reasons why economics has taken its assumptions for granted too long is not the fault of economists. Until they became academic disciplines alongside other disciplines, philosophy and theology had a long tradition of helping society examine assumptions and values. But even as a discipline, theology for one is in a position to help other disciplines become historical-critical and self-critical, because theologians have been forced to do so by the challenge of science. And the sciences themselves have been learning that objectivity is not so easily achieved. A theological and philosophical reading of the history of economics, such as this one, should be able to uncover things that economists have too long taken for granted.[5]

My own assumptions and values are rooted in a worldview shaped by Reformed theology (especially John Calvin) and a process/relational ontology (especially the metaphysics of Alfred North Whitehead and the theology and economics of John B. Cobb Jr.). This is assisted (as is process thought generally) by contemporary developments in the sciences, especially physics and ecology. Fundamental is the belief that the integrity of human life and the health of individual persons depend on the health of communities and ecosystems, because all of reality is inherently and internally related in a seamless web. My judgments about what is problematic about economics and what is promising in economic history are shaped by this worldview—but not dogmatically so, I hope! So are my proposals for ways to transform economics.

These proposals are sketched primarily in the concluding chapter, but my discussion of the contributions of the economists includes much that provides background for the proposals. First and most crucial is for economics to shift from growth in production as its central goal and take up Alfred Marshall's proposed goal of growth in "health and strength." *Homo economicus* should be replaced by *Homo salutaris*, or the "healthy human," and economics should work on measures that compare health and wealth, but make health the priority. Second, both Enlightenment individualism and Marxian socialism need to be succeeded by an anthropology that connects individual freedom and social relations. Human beings need both individuality and participation in community life to be whole persons. The proposal of Herman Daly and John Cobb to develop an anthropology of "persons-in-community" holds promise for economics.[6] Third, I propose that historical-critical method could assist economics in keeping deductive method firmly within proper bounds. Several economists, especially Thomas Malthus and Alfred Marshall, were deeply concerned about the limits of deductive method, but were unable to change its problematic use. (Ironically, though Karl Marx influenced many other disciplines to use historical methods, he did not use this approach in his own economic theory.) Fourth, economics should reconsider the interest of the French Physiocrats in living natural systems; contemporary physics and ecology show more promise as a paradigm for economics than Newtonian mechanics. Finally, a process/relational ontology based on these contemporary sciences is more adequate than the nominalism/voluntarism that undergirds neoclassical economic theory. (Nominalism and voluntarism were philosophies of the Middle Ages that emphasized the distinctness of individual phenomena and the centrality of the individual will—originally, of God's will. They developed in contrast to natural law, which emphasized the relatedness of all of creation, and eventually undermined it by fostering atomistic individualism and freedom as if they could be separate from social relations.) Not only economic theory, but modern Western societies as a whole have become dominated by voluntarism, and have accepted individual choice as the highest value. The solution is not to go back to natural law, which denied individual freedom, but to reconcile the two.

When capitalism is transformed, undifferentiated growth in the production of goods, with no consideration of what kinds of growth, will no longer be the driving goal of economies. The situation now, with rampant growth that is blind to consequences, reminds me of the days in the first half of the twentieth century when "Taylorism," or cookie-cutter production, was the norm for factories. As Henry Ford said, "I don't care what color car they want, as long as it is black." This is the present condition of economics. Economists don't care what kind of growth, as long as the economy grows. Factory production today is far more sophisticated than that, offering customers an endless variety of models and colors and other features. Well, the "customers" of our society want a much more sophisticated economics—one that includes a more complex understanding of "growth" and that safeguards individual, family, community, and ecosystem health. We are saying that something is wrong when we have to choose between jobs and the environment, and between family and work. Of course we have some choices to make ourselves, and many affluent Americans would be healthier if they simplified their lives and worked and consumed less. But our whole society is geared against that, and our economy depends on enormous levels of consumption and work productivity. Many people don't want to have to "drop out" in order to gain a healthier life. We think that economists could do much more to help us move to healthier economic practices and to economies that are environmentally sustainable for our children and grandchildren. There are many useful clues in the history of economics itself that could be used by economists to transform the discipline and ultimately the actual economy. We only need the imagination and the will to do it.

1

For Economic Growth and Individualism over Land: Adam Smith

ALTHOUGH THE HISTORY of the influences that brought modern economics into being is long and complex, the work of Adam Smith (1723–1790) provides a good place to begin. There we can best see the emerging influence and convergence of the three most critical choices for the development of neoclassical economics: the choice to pursue growth in the production of goods as the primary goal of economic activity, the choice to accept the labor theory of value with its correlative emphasis on labor and capital at the expense of land as a unique factor of production, and the choice for individualism. These choices emerge as key elements of Adam Smith's thinking about economic issues, and yet Smith's work is still far from the full development of the consequences of these choices in economic theory and in actual economies. Smith had his head in the modern period, as his monumental *The Wealth of Nations* shows, but his feet were rooted in the more communal past, as is reflected more completely in his earlier and lesser-known work, *The Theory of Moral Sentiments*.

These choices emerged slowly over centuries as key elements of what were to become modern economies. They were not clearly made at any one point by any one person. Still, they were social choices that developed as alternatives to existing patterns and that were accepted and worked for by many influential thinkers over a long period. The first and perhaps most crucial choice, that for economic growth as the single goal of an economy, was perceived as an effective way to escape from the constraints of the land. Since land area was fixed, and after a point more labor on the land did not mean more food produced (the law of diminishing returns), capital and labor were seen as the means to achieve growth. Individualism was thought to be the most efficient way to manage capital and labor.

Adam Smith learned a great deal about economics from his travels in France, but he wrote his great book—*An Inquiry into the Nature and Causes of* the Wealth of Nations—in the context of the early industrialization of Britain. It was a time of reaction against such restrictive practices of mercantilism as emphasizing foreign trade, of hoarding silver and gold as the guarantors of wealth, and of granting monopoly privileges to certain merchants at the expense of others. All of these practices served to keep power in the hands of a few, at a time when an emerging middle class was pushing for the broadening of participation in political and economic life.

At the same time, scientific discovery was providing new ways to interpret social developments. One key image was provided in France by François Quesnay, Madame Pompadour's personal physician. Quesnay used the new image provided by the discovery of the circulation of the blood to express in vivid fashion the emerging idea that economies can grow. He saw that the produce of agriculture and natural resources, as they are circulated and improved by means of processing, provide the means for the increase of national prosperity. Although the economies of Europe had been growing slowly for centuries through the building of towns and their systems of trade, few had clearly seen this before. The idea that the economic base could actually increase, and with proper encouragement, increase enormously, was new. Previously the base of wealth, the landed estates, had simply been taken for granted.

Quesnay and the other French Physiocrats lifted up a dramatic conception of economic growth, as expressed by the Physiocrat Mirabeau:

> The discovery of the *net product*, which we owe to the venerable Confucius of Europe [Quesnay], will one day change the face of the world. . . . The whole moral and physical advantage of societies is . . . summed up in one point, *an increase in the net product;* all damage done to society is determined by this fact, *a reduction in the net product.* It is on the two scales of this balance that you can place and weigh laws, manners, customs, vices, and virtues.[1]

Adam Smith, drawing on the insights of the Physiocrats, and influenced by Newton's new physics, sets out in *The Wealth of Nations* to show that it is indeed this process of economic production and consumption, not the hoarding of metals, that ensures and increases wealth.

Smith differed from the Physiocrats, however, in at least one key respect. The Physiocrats, citizens of a nation dependent on agriculture, saw the land and natural resources not only as the main source of wealth, but as the only source of wealth. Manufacturing, Quesnay insisted, only changes the form of what nature provides; it does not increase it:

> The principle of wealth lies in the source of men's subsistence. Industry prepares wealth for the use of men. One group of men causes this wealth to be generated by means of cultivation; another group prepares it for use; and those who have the enjoyment of it pay both of these groups. If we are to have wealth and men, then, we

must have landed property, men, and wealth. Thus a state which was peopled only with merchants and artisans could subsist only by means of the revenue of the landed property of foreign countries.[2]

Agriculture, then, is the sole source of the net product upon which all progress depends. For the Physiocrats it was the only source of actual economic gain, since land and natural resources are our only source of actual material to work with. Smith, perhaps because he was from a nation much more dependent on trade, looks at the issues from a very different point of view, and accepts a form of the labor theory of value that was most clearly articulated by philosopher John Locke:

> Labour makes the far greatest part of the value of things we enjoy in this world; and the ground which produces the materials is scarce to be reckoned in as any, or at most, but a very small part of it; so little, that even amongst us, land that is left wholly to nature, that hath no improvement of pasturage, tillage, or planting, is called, as indeed it is, waste; and we shall find the benefit of it amount to little more than nothing.[3]

Here we see a clear choice of great consequence, and one that Adam Smith quite consciously made, although one doubts he realized how important it would be. He knew all about the argument of the Physiocrats that wealth depends on the land, and he knew Locke's argument that wealth depends on labor. For his theoretical base, Smith chose labor. He did not deny that agriculture is of very basic importance. But his attention was focused much more on how to increase the productivity of the land and the productivity of labor in manufacturing, not on the more fundamental question of how land, labor, and capital are related in the economy of nature.

Smith was not asking, "What is the source of material wealth and how do we structure our economic activity to protect it?" Land and resources were plentiful—if not in England, then in America, with which England could trade. The problem at the time was not absolute scarcity, but relative scarcity—scarcity of actual goods available for human use. So one may say that the paramount question for Adam Smith was, "What is the means whereby wealth—wealth as goods in hand and available for human use—is increased, and how do we structure our economic activity to make the most of our sources of wealth?" For Smith, as for Locke, if resources remained in a natural state, and thus not immediately available for human use, they might as well be "waste." The bottleneck preventing the generation of abundant wealth for people was not nature itself but the problem of getting at resources and making them usable: hence the focus on the productivity of labor.

Furthermore, Smith chose labor over land in the specific context of the problem of how value is expressed in market price. He did not discuss the three "factors of production"—land, labor, and capital—as such. He did discuss their returns—wages, profits of stock, and rent—but not each factor as a unique element of an economy that must be taken into account on its own terms and in concrete relation to each of the other factors. Smith was not constructing a systematic and consistent theory, and he did not view those factors systematically. He was considering a wide range of problems, and as he went from one to another his focus often shifted considerably. Thus when he focused on the question of determining value in the market, he found the labor theory of value the most convenient; the land appeared to be irrelevant, since the gifts of nature were "free" and the cost was in the "toil and trouble" of extracting resources.[4] But when he focused on the question of developing a healthy national economy, Smith was adamant about the fundamental importance of agriculture, as we shall see.[5]

Smith did agree with the Physiocrats that the greatest source of productivity gain is indeed in agriculture, because there "nature labours along with man," and he contended that a wise nation will develop its agriculture first, and then turn to manufacturing and trade, because of the greater productivity of agriculture. "No equal quantity of productive labour employed in manufactures can ever occasion so great a reproduction. In them nature does nothing; man does all; and the reproduction must always be in proportion to the strength of the agents that occasion it."[6]

Smith asserts that any nation prospers best by beginning its development with domestic agriculture and then domestic manufacturing for domestic consumption. Only after these basics are achieved does it make sense to move into exporting the surplus:

> When the capital of any country is not sufficient for all those three purposes, in proportion as a greater share of it is employed in agriculture, the greater will be the quantity of productive labour which it puts into motion within the country; as will likewise be the value which its employment adds to the annual produce of the land and labour of the society. After agriculture, the capital employed in manufactures puts into motion the greatest quantity of productive labour, and adds the greatest value to the annual produce. That which is employed in the trade of exportation, has the least effect of any of the three.[7]

Smith goes on to explain that capital employed in trade is the least productive simply because foreign trade splits the use of capital between the home country and the other country:

> The capital which sends British goods to Portugal, and brings back Portuguese goods to Great Britain, replaces by every such operation only one British capital. The

other is a Portuguese one. Though the returns, therefore, of the foreign trade of consumption should be as quick as those of the home-trade, the capital employed in it will give but one-half the encouragement to the industry or productive labour of the country.[8]

The reason for concentrating on agriculture first was not just that it was the most efficient place to begin in terms of producing goods. It was, Smith believed, also a matter of beginning with basic "necessities" first, and only then branching out to produce for "conveniencies and luxuries":

As subsistence is, in the nature of things, prior to conveniency and luxury, so the industry which procures the former, must necessarily be prior to that which ministers to the latter. The cultivation and improvement of the country, therefore, which affords subsistence, must, necessarily, be prior to the increase of the town, which furnishes only the means of conveniency and luxury. It is the surplus produce of the country only, or what is over and above the maintenance of the cultivators, that constitutes the subsistence of the town, which can therefore increase only with the increase of this surplus produce. . . .

That order of things which necessity imposes in general, though not in every particular country, is, in every particular country, promoted by the natural inclinations of man. If human institutions had never thwarted those natural inclinations, the towns could no-where have increased beyond what the improvement and cultivation of the territory in which they were situated could support; till such time, at least, as the whole of that territory was completely cultivated and improved.[9]

The "natural inclinations" that Smith is referring to are those of preferring the security, independence, and even beauty of cultivating the land to the uncertainty of manufacture and trade.[10] Smith cannot imagine a world in which life on the land would be despised, and where "necessities" would not be prior to "conveniency and luxury."

Smith's famous passage about the "invisible hand" that brings about the best outcome in a market where each individual is left free to participate or not, is actually a discussion of his assertion that it is more advantageous to the wealth of both individuals and nations that capital should be employed domestically, and sent abroad only when no profitable use can be found for it at home. This critical context of his theory of the "invisible hand" has been overlooked. Contemporary economic theory typically celebrates complete individual freedom to employ capital wherever the individual pleases as an unquestioned recipe for economic success. Yet Smith's argument for individual liberty assumes that it is quite safe to leave individuals free in this fashion only because national interest and individual interest happen to be the same:

He saves himself the risk and trouble of exportation, when, so far as he can, he thus converts his foreign trade of consumption into a home-trade. Home is in this manner the center, if I may say so, round which the capitals of the inhabitants of every country are continually circulating, and towards which they are always tending. . . . A capital employed in the home-trade, it has already been shown, necessarily puts into motion a greater quantity of domestic industry, and gives revenue and employment to a greater number of the inhabitants of the country, than an equal capital employed in the foreign trade. . . . Upon equal, or only nearly equal profits, therefore, every individual naturally inclines to employ his capital in the manner in which it is likely to afford the greatest support to domestic industry, and to give revenue and employment to the greatest number of people of his own country.[11]

With this last comment, however, it appears that Smith does not see the potential consequence of what he is saying. He goes on to argue for free trade as advantageous to the national wealth, but he assumes that trade will be a matter of investing capital abroad that would not be efficiently used at home, and thus is really surplus to the domestic economy. It does not seem to occur to him here that, if profits are not "equal, or only nearly equal," but higher abroad, then capital might be drained from domestic use that would, from the point of view of giving "revenue and employment to a greater number of the inhabitants of the country," be better employed at home. Later theorists, using maximum profits as their sole indicator of economic "efficiency," would see no problem with the exportation of capital, irrespective of the consequences to domestic employment that Smith thought important.

Although Smith does clearly see the importance of agriculture to newly developing nations, such as those in North America in his day, he concentrated much more on the situation of Britain, where agriculture was more developed and the law of diminishing returns had already come into play (whereby more labor applied to the land did not increase production proportionately). Even though improvements were being made in agriculture, economic growth depended much more on trade and the embryonic manufacturing sector, where technical innovation and new markets offered much more scope for development. Most of Smith's discussion assumes this situation, but later theorists simply abstracted from it and then applied the abstracted theory to the very different situation of newly developing agricultural nations without taking the difference of context into account.

The idea of beginning economic development by concentrating on domestic agriculture to develop domestic markets, and only later moving to foreign trade and manufacture for export, has been largely ignored in contemporary development schemes. It is more typical for nations to invest large amounts of capital in industrial development for export, and to use agriculture and natural resources for the same purpose in order to earn foreign exchange for further investment.[12] This "top-down," export-driven mode of development has been followed by Brazil and Mexico, to give two examples. Although they have indeed grown tremendously by economic measures, they also have acquired massive debt loads, accompanied by a downward spiral of increasing exports destroying forests and degrading cropland while squeezing out small farmers who grow for domestic consumption. It may also be important to distinguish between export-driven development that concentrates on exporting finished manufactured goods—such as has been the case in Japan, South Korea, Taiwan, and Singapore—and export-driven development that relies on the export of unfinished raw materials, as has occurred in the Philippines and Malaysia.

The few nations that have followed the mode of development suggested by Smith have, by contrast, developed with spectacular successes, Japan being the most famous example, followed closely by South Korea and Taiwan. Peter Berger, in his book *The Capitalist Revolution*, repeatedly cites the emphasis on radical land reform and improvement of domestic agriculture as foundational to the success of East Asian capitalist development.[13] While it is not my purpose here to analyze contemporary modes of economic development, it is important to show how Smith's way of thinking about the issues raises questions that should be pursued. The success of the Asian "tigers," compared with the much more uneven development of many Latin American nations, might well prove an example of how economic theory (both neoclassical capitalist and Marxian), which focused blindly on "growth" with no consideration of what kind of growth and for what purpose in what context, has through ahistoric and "scientific" application of theory missed crucial opportunities to distinguish between types of economic development. If these differences had been carefully delineated early on, both theoretically and politically, many developing countries might have avoided problems. Adam Smith, though his theory was messier, may have been wiser.

The decline of attention to the land also had political grounds. The land was controlled by the nobility, both in France and in England. The Physiocrats, intent on the importance of the land, tended to get politically entangled in supporting the nobility. They accepted the *ancien régime* and the principle of absolute monarchy, hoping to effect top-down reform of the system that everyone agreed was no longer functioning. When Robert Turgot, a fellow traveler with the Physiocrats, briefly held power as Louis XIV's minister of finance, he tried to carry out these reforms, including abolishing local monopolies and fiscal abuses, the hated *corvée* (forced labor), internal duties, and excessive and unfair taxation—all of which were disincentives to improving and caring for the land.[14] Turgot's suggested reforms would have been helpful if they had not been too late. The French Revolution swept away the great landowners and discredited the Physiocrats. Their politics went down, and with it their ideas about the inherent importance of land and resources. Ironically, they had tried to convince the wrong party, the nobility; their ideas would have been far more useful to the revolutionaries—who of course would have nothing to do with them, since they had backed the wrong side.

Adam Smith picked up their idea about *net produit* and economic growth, and although he accepted the importance of agriculture, he was much more concerned with manufacture and trade. And though his discussion of concrete problems was frequently informed, empirically based, and full of wisdom—as generations of readers have attested—his lack of theoretical clarity was unfortunate. It was left for David Ricardo to achieve clarity for economic theory, and in doing so Ricardo omitted at the theoretical level some of the implications of Smith's observations about what healthy economic development needs to include. If the focus had been on the question of a healthy economy, which served "necessities" and community needs first, rather than on economic growth in abstraction from the question of health, the theory would have developed differently, and land would not have disappeared as a key and unique factor.

More important than theoretical considerations was the politics of the land. The emerging middle class, or bourgeoisie, was pressing for greater participation in national life, both economically and politically. That meant resisting the power of the great merchant monopolies, and it meant resisting the great landholding nobility, who had ensured with the "Corn Laws" that they would receive high rents. The Corn Laws forbade or placed high tariffs on the import of grain to protect domestic production. Consequently, wages had to be higher to provide subsistence for labor, and so manufacturing was inhibited. This situation was fodder for a bitter battle that lasted well into the 1840s, and its consequences for the development of economics—both capitalist and Marxian—were enormous. That story comes in more fully when we discuss Malthus, Ricardo, and Marx, but here we need to see the intense political reasons, which operated from the outset, for the way land was considered in the development of economics. Indeed, land has not really been considered in its own right in economic discourse since the Physiocrats were politically discredited two hundred years ago.

Smith begins *The Wealth of Nations* with a discussion of how the productivity of labor can be improved. In his time the bottleneck in the generation of wealth was clearly the limited productivity of labor. He observes that in "the savage nations of hunters and fishers," where everyone who can work does, there is great poverty, while in "civilized" nations many do not work at all, and yet "all are often abundantly supplied, and a man, even of the lowest and poorest order, if he is frugal and industrious, may enjoy a greater share of the necessaries and conveniencies of life than it is possible for any savage to acquire."[15] Smith is famous for pointing out how it is that "civilized" nations can so much more effectively produce goods than "savage" ones: by means of the division and specialization of labor. He shows in his classic description of the production of the pin factory how this works, and thus how productive efficiency depends on labor efficiency, which depends on specialization and division and on technological innovation.[16]

Smith was quite right about his central issue, the production of goods. But assumptions he makes along the way reveal which values he was selecting, which values he was taking for granted, and which values were being denied or ignored. Clearly, the value that Smith elevates is that of producing more of the "necessities, conveniencies, and amusements of human life."[17] He assumes that when more is produced, everyone, even "of the lowest and poorest," can gain more goods, and that this is of the greatest priority because "savage" nations "are so miserably poor, that from mere want are frequently reduced, or, at least, think themselves reduced, of necessity sometimes of directly destroying, and sometimes of abandoning their infants, their old people, and those afflicted with lingering diseases, to perish with hunger, or to be devoured by wild beasts."[18]

Smith gives no documentation for these assertions; they are simply the commonly accepted understanding of his day. Because of his assumption, discussed above, that necessities will be met first, he does not need to distinguish between production geared to necessities and production geared to luxuries.

The assumption that necessities come first no longer holds in economic theory, but this theory still teaches that sheer maximization of the production of goods is the best way to improve the lot of the poor. When confronted with the high cost of industrial development in terms of cultural and community breakdown and the mass misery of laborers, both economists and political policy makers typically argue for the benefits of capitalism in the long run on the basis that its productive efficiency eventually outweighs a few generations of dislocation and misery. Peter Berger explains the famous theory of economist Simon Kuznets that "as modern economic growth continues over time, there occurs first a sharp rise in inequality and then, later, a leveling effect." He goes on to assert: "There is widespread agreement today that, to date, the hypothesis has been confirmed, both historically and cross-nationally."[19]

It is assumed that the people affected by industrialization prefer in the long run to increase the number of goods available to them, even at the cost of the integrity of their culture and their communities. Rarely has this question been seriously addressed. When I have raised it among economists and others, it has usually been dismissed with a remark to the effect that obviously everyone but idealistic romantics prefers goods to traditional culture, and "better jobs" in the city to dull, hard labor on the farm. Berger writes at length about the material and physical miseries of premodern life, in the millennia before the industrial revolution:

> It is important to keep in mind the long-lasting realities of material life so as to avoid the recurring romanticisms about premodern times. As a mental exercise, for example, one might focus on the fact that almost all of human history took place without the benefits of modern dentistry. This means, quite simply, that most individuals either suffered from toothaches or had rotten teeth; it probably means that their mouths both looked and smelled accordingly.[20]

Everyone, it would seem, has accepted the mythology that all premodern life was inherently lived in miserable poverty and cultural stupidity. (Berger does admit that "cultural stupidity" is a myth, but many apologists for both capitalism and socialism do not.) Only fairly recently have anthropologists begun to question this picture of traditional hunter-gatherer societies, and of some of the less ancient agricultural societies such as the Maya of southeastern Mexico, through careful studies of the few such groups that still exist and the remains of past groups. They are discovering that the picture painted of premodern societies as always miserably poor and unhealthy, which Adam Smith and nearly everyone else accepted without question, is indeed mistaken.

Some premodern societies, including traditional hunter-gatherers, some nomadic peoples, and some types of agricultural communities (before they began to be crowded off good land by more aggressive "civilized" peoples), lived in a fashion that was by and large healthier and more "abundant" in many measures, including food, than that of many peoples living today. They were tall, showing that they had adequate protein, and they did not lose their teeth, showing that they had healthy, balanced diets. They had sophisticated oral cultures and a wealth of knowledge about their local ecosystems that scientists today are drawing upon. For example, in the Amazon basin medical researchers have discovered that practitioners of traditional medicine can save them years of trial-and-error research on rain-forest plants to find those of medical benefit. These "savages" have already done generations of research and can often lead Western researchers right to what they are seeking.

Even life in the Stone Age is being viewed differently. In a book of essays on current anthropology, Marvin Harris describes Stone Age life this way:

> The first flaw in this theory is the assumption that life was exceptionally difficult for our stone age ancestors. Archaeological evidence from the upper paleolithic period—about 30,000 b.c. to 10,000 b.c.—makes it perfectly clear that hunters who lived during those times enjoyed relatively high standards of comfort and security. They were no bumbling amateurs. . . . , and they have aptly been called the "master

stoneworkers of all times.". . . . Contrary to popular ideas, "cave men" knew how to make artificial shelters. . . . With rich furs for rugs and beds, as well as plenty of dried animal dung or fat-laden bones for the hearth, such dwellings can provide a quality of shelter superior in many respects to contemporary inner-city apartments.

As for living on the edge of starvation, such a picture is hard to reconcile with the enormous quantities of animal bones accumulated at various paleolithic kill sites. . . . Moreover, the skeletal remains of the hunters themselves bear witness to the fact that they were unusually well-nourished.

The notion that paleolithic populations worked round the the clock in order to feed themselves now also appears ludicrous.[21]

Harris goes on to assert that before agriculture was introduced, work itself was not necessarily hard and endless. "The development of farming resulted in an increased work load per capita." And he concludes that:

As long as population density—and thus exploitation of these resources—is kept relatively low, hunter-collectors can enjoy both leisure and high-quality diets. Only if one assumes that people during the stone age were unwilling or unable to limit the density of their populations does the theory of our ancestors' lives as "short, nasty, and brutish" make sense. But that assumption is unwarranted. Hunter-collectors are strongly motivated to limit population, and they have effective means to do so.[22]

What does this seeming digression have to do with Adam Smith and the history of economics? Everything. If we had understood traditional cultures better all along, we might have asked different questions and seen different choices. Because hunting and gathering societies were thought of as "savage" and "miserably poor" (perhaps because the groups that were observed had already been decimated by Western diseases and encroachment on their lands), and because the agricultural communities that were considered were also poor and seen to be "idiotic," to use Marx's term, it was easy to dismiss concern for the disintegration of traditional and rural communities as foolish romanticism that was blind to the real misery of life on the land.

There was concern. It was expressed by the people directly affected, when they protested the rise of the factory system and the loss of their own access to the land through the enclosure of the common lands. It was expressed by the whole romantic movement in literature and by its corollary utopian socialist movement. Although these latter movements came after Adam Smith, he should have been well aware of the protests of the people against enclosure and the misery of factory work. Yet Smith does not talk about these issues. He is aware that factory work, when specialization goes too far, is monotonous, and he advocates liberal wages for labor as good for the economy.[23] But reading *The Wealth of Nations*, one is struck by the amount of abstraction from the concrete situation of Britain, and especially Scotland, that Smith engages in. Unlike John Stuart Mill—who takes care to describe at length concrete economies, such as that of Switzerland—Smith does not describe the overall economic situation of his time. All around him, the Scots people, especially in the Highlands, were suffering the impact of the enclosure of their lands and the persecution imposed by the English government, in the wake of the 1745 defeat of the Jacobites, against their language, culture, economy, and political traditions. Thousands were forced to emigrate from their ancestral lands, and they expressed themselves in song and poetry as having been betrayed and ruined by the greed of a few for "riches."[24]

None of this distress is visible in *The Wealth of Nations*. Smith simply accepts the beginning economic trends toward urbanization and factory labor without serious question. He seems to have no idea, or does not find it at all problematic, that so many people are being forced to accept a choice for their lives that someone else has made. He believes strongly that the mass of people are clearly better off in factory labor than they were in rural life, because the amount and quality of goods available to them has increased:

> The real recompense of labour, the real quantity of the necessaries and conveniencies of life which it can procure to the labourer, has, during the course of the present century, increased perhaps in a still greater proportion than its money price. Not only grain has become somewhat cheaper, but many other things. . . . The great improvements in the coarser manufactures of both linen and woolen cloth furnish the labourers with cheaper and better cloathing . . . as well as with many agreeable and convenient pieces of household furniture.[25]

There is no disputing this. Goods were becoming available to the masses that most had never dreamed of. Yet the people themselves, while welcoming the goods, questioned the consequences. It was not unusual for people to work for large portions of the year away from home in order to be able to continue to live in their traditional villages.

In the 1800s Scottish commentators remarked with puzzlement that these laborers seemed determined to live as they always had, despite years of contact with more "advanced" and more "abundant" ways of life.[26] In his social-economic history of Scotland, scholar T. C. Smout, writing in 1986, comments on this:

> What was surprising to men like McNeill [a nineteenth-century observer] was that so many Highlanders refused either to accept their removal as inevitable or to interpret it as a chance for betterment. Had not Adam Smith spoken, in a well-known phrase, of "the uniform, constant and uninterrupted effort of every man to better his own condition"? It followed that, in pursuit of self-interest, no Highlander should have

hesitated to migrate to a locality like East Lothian where there were jobs to be had, and that eviction should never have been necessary. But Gaelic Highlanders often refused to conform to the model of Smithian man.[27]

It is indicative of the state of our cultural understanding that Smout, when he speculates on the reason for the Highlander's odd attachment to traditional life, never once considers that the Highlander has chosen to value community life more than individual "gain."

The question that Smith did not raise, and none of the great historic economists we will examine (including Marx) raised, is this: Might it not have been possible to achieve greater efficiency in the production of goods without so disrupting community life and culture? This is no rhetorical question put to dead history, but a matter of contemporary urgency. There are still places in the world that have not yet been transformed by capitalist or Marxist industrialization. Millions of people look at the economic choices offered them and ask if they want to bear the cost in the destruction of their cultures and communities.

This brings us to the third choice that emerges with Adam Smith, though it does not reach its full development until the late 1800s. That is the choice for individualism. Critics often read twentieth-century views of individualism back into Smith and miss the context of social relations that Smith assumed for it, described in *The Theory of Moral Sentiments*.[28] But Smith's view is definitely individualistic, despite the context of social relations that he describes for human beings. Smith's assumption that individualism reigns in nature, and is ameliorated in human society, shows that he places individualism ontologically prior to social relations:

> The difference between the most dissimilar characters, between a philosopher and a common street porter, for example, seems to arise not so much from nature, as from habit, custom, and education.
>
> Each animal is still obliged to support and defend itself, separately and independently, and derives no sort of advantage from that variety of talents with which nature has distinguished its fellows. Among men, on the contrary, the most dissimilar geniuses are of use to one another; the different products of their respective talents, by the general disposition to truck, barter, and exchange, being brought, as it were, into a common stock, where every man may purchase whatever part of the produce of other men's talents for which he has occasion.[29]

Smith was wrong about individualism in nature. Animals do indeed derive great benefit from the "variety of talents" that distinguishes them, and they have complex social relations of their own. The important point is that, although Smith's description of how individuals actually participate in society in many respects assumes the importance of social relations, he still accepted for his theoretical base the individualism of the Enlightenment era. In the long run theoretical individualism was to have more impact on the development of Western culture and economies than his recommendations about specific concrete economic issues, such as the healthiest way to develop a nation's economy.

Enlightenment individualism was based on Newtonian physics, which assumed that the world is composed of discrete, independently existing individual entities. In this atomistic individualism, relations between entities are strictly external—they exist as they are whether they have any relationships or not. It is important to understand that Enlightenment thinkers, as they considered the meaning of Newtonian physics for their understanding of the world, believed that the individualism they were promoting in social relations was not a matter of social choice but rather simply a matter of getting in tune with the way the world actually is. This was the basis of their faith in what they called "natural liberty," or "natural law."

Like the Catholic promoters of natural law in earlier centuries, the Enlightenment thinkers thought positive law should be in line with natural law. But the content of the natural law was radically changed by Newton's new physics. Catholic natural law, based on Aristotelian physics, saw the world as a unified hierarchy in which every entity is related to every other entity by virtue of its place in the hierarchy. Thus society functions best, and individuals are fulfilled, when everyone accepts his or her designated place and role. Ethics tended to be a matter of figuring out where everyone was supposed to be, and how to get those given power to treat those under them with justice. But the hierarchy of nature itself was created by God and could not be questioned.

This view of the social task as one of conforming to the dictates of "natural law" was of course changing for a very long time before Newton, even as society was changing (and the preceding development of nominalism/voluntarism in philosophy and theology played a major role). But Newton gave philosophers a new basis, grounded in science, for radically changing the old understanding of natural law. The Enlightenment thinkers rejected the old view of nature as a hierarchy of fixed, inherent relations. Following Newton, they believed that nature is composed not of inherently related entities but of independent entities, which related through such external "laws of nature" as gravity. This new version of natural law theory was loaded with inconsistencies and confusions. For instance, Enlightenment philosophers never figured out how to account for human freedom when the rest of nature is bound by externally imposed iron laws, nor, on the other hand, how to account for causation in nature itself when entities are supposedly self-existent and independent.

In the midst of all the confusion, one premise is fairly consistent: things existing in nature are coerced by externally imposed laws into behaving according to those laws. This premise was accepted by Enlightenment thinkers for nature, and this seems to have meant to them that human relations can be of two kinds: either coerced by externally imposed laws, analogously to the workings of the laws of nature, or voluntarily entered into. Smith certainly prefers the latter, in company with Locke, Hume, and his other Enlightenment mentors. But none of them explains how it can be safe to leave relations to voluntary behavior. They assert that "natural liberty" leads people to choose what is best for them, and what is best for individuals is best for the whole society, but their grounds for making this optimistic assertion are slight indeed. In Smith I can find no firmer ground for it than the observation that it is in the best interest of businesspeople to invest at home rather than abroad. Even Smith is aware, however, that businesspeople will easily move their capital away if they can get greater profit elsewhere. "A merchant, it has been said very properly, is not necessarily the citizen of any particular country. It is in a great measure indifferent to him from what place he carries on his trade; and a very trifling disgust will make him remove his capital, and together with it all the industry which it supports, from one country to another."[30]

Here Smith's inconsistency shows up most clearly. He has no illusions here about the domestic loyalty of capitalists, yet in other parts of the work he happily asserts that they will certainly prefer to employ their "capitals" at home.[31] At any rate, the safety of leaving economic and political matters to "natural liberty" seems to be based mostly on faith in the new Newtonian view.

Applied to societies, Enlightenment natural law theory meant that human beings were considered first as individuals whose relations were external to their existence, but who would "naturally" enter into relationships for their own advantage. Social relations were thus not divinely fixed but mandated by human choice (which opened the door politically for democratic societies to develop). Because natural law would lead humans to the best outcome, as gravity works naturally on physical bodies, it was safe, and indeed preferable, to leave individuals to work out their relations for themselves, rather than try to impose alien "positive" laws that often worked against natural forces. Because individual self-interest by "nature" was in line with social interest, there was no need to worry about sin. Even selfish individuals would inevitably contribute to society, even without intending to do so, because of this correspondence of individual and social interest. This is Smith's famous description of this phenomenon:

> As every individual, therefore, endeavours as much as he can both to employ his capital in the support of domestic industry, and so to direct that industry that its produce may be of the greatest value; every individual necessarily labours to render the annual revenue of the society as great as he can. He generally, indeed, neither intends to promote the public interest, nor knows how much he is promoting it. By preferring the support of domestic to that of foreign industry, he intends only his own

security; and by directing that industry in such a manner as its produce may be of the greatest value, he intends only his own gain, and he is in this, as in many other cases, led by an invisible hand to promote an end which was no part of his intention. Nor is it always the worse for the society that it was no part of it. By pursuing his own interest he frequently promotes that of the society more effectually than when he really intends to promote it. I have never known much good done by those who affected to trade for the public good.[32]

Adam Smith does not articulate this theory as clearly as contemporary economists do, but I think the contemporary development, which asserts that individuals should be left free to pursue their own self-interest, is a fair interpretation of what he assumed to be the case.

Nevertheless, what Smith articulates for his theory is once again somewhat different from what he says when discussing actual social relations, and he does not see the consequences of the theory when abstracted from those social relations. Contemporary neoclassical economic theory focuses on the freedom of individuals to compete in the market, with the accent on the *competition* of individuals acting solely for their own self-interest. But Adam Smith did not focus on competition so much as on individual *participation* in the market. Although much has been made of Smith's discussions of individual liberty, little attention has been given to the dimension of increasing participation—which for Smith was a most important part of the meaning of liberty. Thus the individualism of Adam Smith was very different from the individualism that emerged later.

When Smith argued for a free market, with individuals left free to decide how to participate, he was arguing against the kind of central control that mercantilism had exerted by means of monopoly grants (including local monopolies), guild control of crafts, city control of a particular export, and the like. His argument was based not so much on the idea that competition was more efficient than monopoly (at least not in the sense meant by twentieth-century neoclassical economic theory), as on the belief that the results of free participation by everyone concerned in decision making about what and how much to produce and how to price it in the market would be much more efficient than control by central authorities.

Smith observed that no central authority could possibly have the kind of local knowledge and local relationships that are required to take best advantage of local conditions of supply and demand. Only the people on the spot can have that kind of detailed knowledge and can make the necessary arrangements for producing, hauling, and selling with maximum efficiency: "What is the species of domestic industry which his capital can employ, and of which the produce is likely to be of the greatest value, every individual, it is evident, can, in his local situation, judge much better than any statesman or lawgiver can do for him."[33]

It was clear to Smith that when local people are allowed to participate directly in the economic decisions that affect them, they do so with more wisdom and more efficient tailoring of production to demand in the market than do central authorities (or small minorities in command of local monopolies). Contemporary renderings of Smith's observations of his local Scottish market have tended to emphasize the elements of individualism and competition in Smith's description, though more recent textbooks are getting more careful.[34] He never assumed that it would be safe to allow consistently selfish behavior by all the individuals competing in the market, just because competition would ensure a beneficial outcome. Consistent with his earlier *Theory of Moral Sentiments*, which argued for the importance of the broader social context and social relations, Smith's argument for the free market depended on the assumption that even selfish individuals would be restrained by their neighbors from cheating, price fixing, and the like, because of the reality of social relations that make honest behavior correspond with self-interest: "The real and effectual discipline which is exercised over a workman, is not that of his corporation, but that of his customers. It is the fear of losing their employment which restrains his frauds and corrects his negligence."[35]

The market that Adam Smith describes, in which the paticipants are free to work out how to balance supply and demand for themselves, is not more efficient than a "command" market simply because of individual competition and individual decisions. As one textbook puts it, the price system "shows decision making to be decentralized under the control of millions of individual producers and consumers but nonetheless to be coordinated."[36] This seems to assume that if there is no central, single source of coordination, then there is no "planned or intentional" coordination at all. Yet the market works through the intentional actions of many, who coordinate with each other how they want to go about coping with demand and supply.

Suppose, then, that while individual competition is a factor, free markets are also more efficient because of very personalized participation, which creates the more efficient web of local relationships that in turn makes possible more specific and quicker adjustments to market signals than central authorities can make. All the participants adapt themselves to each other and make arrangements with each other to keep their part of production or selling going in relation to the other parts. This web of relations extends throughout the market system: what is happening at one end quickly affects the reaction at the other end, even when the participants at each end of the network do not know each other.

The important factor, however, is not that they do not know each other. Too much is made of "impersonal competition," as if businesses and consumers react only to price signals. The "invisible sea of relations" in which all the participants swim is at least as important. Smith was well aware of this.[37] He was not arguing for impersonal competition versus central control but for what would actually be more personal involvement by all the individuals concerned instead of the less personal and less efficient central control. Smith was right that no central source of "control" can possibly negotiate the complexity of the system as well as each of the participants can. Later versions of the "invisible hand" theory of market mechanisms concentrate on price signals as crucial— and indeed, as the only really important issue for understanding why free markets are more efficient than externally controlled markets.[38] Yet nothing in Smith's description requires this interpretation. Instead, it is possible to read Smith as more interested in making market relations internal to the system by freeing the participants to make their own decisions, rather than continuing the external imposition of order by nonparticipants who are making decisions for political or other reasons that have nothing to do with the best way to keep the market running smoothly. Although it was thought that only a single source of control could prevent chaos, Smith showed how coherence could emerge from the interactions of many such centers, so that power could be shared with positive results. (It is interesting that computer systems are now designed on this same principle, with many "independently" functioning parts instead of the traditional central processing chip controlling everything. These new systems work much faster and can handle many more tasks.)

Adam Smith, then, presents us with a rich mix of ideas about how to achieve the single goal he chose for economics: growth in the production of goods. It is conceivable that economic theory would have developed quite differently if later economists had chosen to pay more attention to such issues as the role of agriculture, the viability and health of communities (human and natural), and the importance of maximizing participation as another way of thinking about how to overcome the limitations of central control. But the next stage in the development of economics was dominated by David Ricardo, and his choice of deductive method, with individualism and growth enshrined in the method's assumptions, set the direction of economics decisively.

2

For Deductive Method and Rent over Poor Relief: David Ricardo and Thomas Malthus

ADAM SMITH sorted out some key dimensions of economics in a way that made it possible to consider economic questions systematically and somewhat abstracted from the whole welter of social, political, economic, cultural, and environmental factors. Earlier writers treating economic problems might have achieved clarity on one issue or another, and the Physiocrats tried to treat the economy as a system in its own right. It is because their "system" was not accepted, and Smith's was, that Smith gets the credit for developing economics as a science. His thinking has had the greatest impact and his fundamental insights have not yet been superseded.

The next crucial stage that we will consider in the development of economics came with the work of two writers, David Ricardo (1772–1823) and Thomas Malthus (1766–1834). Malthus was an Anglican minister who happened to be interested in economic problems as part of the social problems of his day. Ricardo was a businessman who was interested in bringing more clarity to economics as a system. Ironically, it was the work of the businessman that Marx was able to use in his crusade for the working class, and it was the work of the clergyman that Marx condemned as antilabor. For in the controversy over the Corn Laws and the origins of rent, Ricardo showed an alliance between interests of labor and capital against the landlords, while Malthus defended the the landlords. This controversy had an important impact on the question of "land" as a unique resource. Worse, Malthus elaborated his theory of population (which showed that population growth can easily outstrip growth in food supply) just at the time when it could be used to great effect against "poor relief," as we shall see. The theory of population and the resulting fear of the consequences of an economic "stationary state" provided tremendous impetus to the choice for growth.

One might think that the impact of Malthus's theory of population on the social treatment of the poor would raise the most important value questions for this stage of the development of economic theory. Indeed it did have a long-term impact on the development of economic theory and world economies. But the crucial value choice made at this stage concerned an entirely different matter, and has been almost universally acclaimed rather than questioned. This was the choice made by Ricardo to pursue clarity at all costs—to make of economics a "science" based on deductive method.

Ricardo made economics a science by limiting its scope to issues that can be treated by means of deductive scientific methods. Deduction depends on the choice of a few basic assumptions that constitute one's operating theoretical framework, the formulation of a theory from that framework, and the application of the resulting theory to the problems at hand. The implications or predictions of the theory are tested by the gathering of data, but the foundational assumptions, once established and accepted, are rarely reconsidered until or unless the data are simply too different too often from what the theory leads scientists to expect. The purpose of deductive method is to make it possible for scientists to cope with the enormous complexities of reality by choosing carefully only particular aspects of it that are of interest and importance.

Consider, as a parallel example, how our eyes function. Human vision, like deductive method, already has built-in, preselected biases. Human eyes do not see the full spectrum of light, but only a rather narrow range of the spectrum, which provides us with only a particular range of information. This range makes it possible for humans to perceive clearly what it is most crucial to perceive: whether the patch of brown over there is a tree or a bear, for instance. Not only is the fact that thousands of other things are going on at the same time not relevant to the immediate problem of survival, but attention to much of that other data would only overload our capacity to cope. Our eyes, then, do not so much bring us information as screen it out, allowing us to concentrate on what evolution has determined to be crucial for survival.

Similarly, deductive method allows scientists to "screen out" most of the welter of possible data, and to select only those types of data that are of crucial interest. In scientific laboratories it is possible to conduct controlled experiments in which only one or two factors are changed at a time while everything else is kept the same. (This is called ceteris paribus: "other things being equal.") Like eyesight, deductive method has proved to be a powerful tool that brings great clarity to scientific analysis. This has been true also in economics, although economics has the disadvantage of being impossible to do in a laboratory. Real economies cannot be isolated (and controlled) for experimental purposes from the rest of the social, cultural, political, and environmental matrix of life. But deductive method did make it possible to focus attention on particular activities that were relevant to specifically economic problems in a way that had not been done with such clarity before.

Ricardo's use of deductive method made it possible to remove many of the "confusions" in Smith's work. For example, we saw in chapter 1 how Smith argued for free trade, yet also held that the domestic employment of capital is better for a nation's economic growth than foreign trade is. Ricardo, using the sharp tools of analysis, was able to show that the confusion lay in not understanding what was to be called "the principle of comparative advantage." Instead of trying to consider trade in terms of all the various goods exported and imported, along with the implications for the money supply, Ricardo simplified the issue for the purpose of clarity, and considered the situation of England trading wool cloth to Portugal in exchange for wine.[1]

Ricardo was able to show that even if it were cheaper (measured in labor time) for Portugal to make both cloth and wine than to import cloth from England, it would still be in Portugal's interest to import cloth and export wine if Portugal's advantage in making wine was greater than its advantage in making cloth. Portugal would then be using its productive capacity more efficiently, and England, which could make wool cloth comparatively more efficiently than wine, would be doing the same. Thus England has a comparative advantage in the production of cloth, even though Portugal has an absolute advantage in cloth as well as wine. This makes it worthwhile for England and Portugal to trade wool cloth and wine with each other, rather than to make them for themselves. Ricardo's conclusion was that free trade leads to the more efficient use of the productive resources of land, capital, and labor. Smith was judged wrong for thinking that domestic investment was inherently more productive for a nation than trade—especially trade in goods that made the subsistence of laborers cheaper to achieve.[2]

Since Ricardo's elaboration of the theory of comparative advantage in 1817, free trade has become a cherished tenet of capitalist economists. The theory of comparative advantage is a key element of today's neoclassical theory, applied worldwide, or at least argued for worldwide by capitalist economists. Once Ricardo was able, by isolating a few key elements of the problem of trade for attention, to understand the dynamic of comparative advantage, the hypothesis was included in the growing body of economic theory and helped to give the theory "scientific" status.

Once the theory of comparative advantage became part of the classical economic model, attention to the historical context in which Ricardo observed the phenomenon was thought to be no longer necessary. Economists have continued to apply the theory in changed circumstances, without realizing the implications. When Ricardo described the mutual benefits of trade between England and Portugal, he was careful to stipulate that the reciprocal advantage depended on the fact that capital and labor did not flow freely between the two nations, but only the products—wool cloth and wine:

It would undoubtedly be advantageous to the capitalists of England, and to the consumers in both countries, that under such circumstances [when both products could be made more cheaply in Portugal] the wine and the cloth should both be made in Portugal, and therefore that the capital and labour of England employed in making cloth should be removed to Portugal for that purpose. In that case, the relative value of these commodities would be regulated by the same principle as if one were the produce of Yorkshire and the other of London: and in every other case, if capital freely flowed towards those countries where it could be most profitably employed, there could be no difference in the rate of profit, and no other difference in the real or labour price of commodities than the additional quantity of labour required to convey them to the various markets where they were to be sold.[3]

The theory of comparative advantage depends on a situation in which capital and labor do not flow freely between nations, and in which there is a difference between the rate of profit and the level of wages in the countries concerned. If capital and labor do flow freely, then the situation is like that between Yorkshire and London: If labor is cheaper in London and both wool and wine can be produced more cheaply there, then capital investment will flow to London, and both wool cloth and wine will be produced there. Yorkshire will both lose labor to London and be forced to lower its wages until it has the same level of wages and rate of profit as London.

Is this not a good thing? With free trade, will not the whole world eventually have the same level of wages and rate of profit, so that everyone can trade on the same basis? Well, yes, but what will that level of wages be? Suppose that investors move their capital around from nation to nation to find the lowest possible level of wages. A poor nation like the Philippines, desperate for jobs at any price, will not only allow investors to pay subsistence wages but will compromise its environmental integrity in order to attract and keep foreign investment in the country. When labor begins to organize and demand a larger share, and when more people begin to demand greater respect for the environment, the corporations can pull out and invest in another, more desperate nation—and the economic incentives to maximize profits push corporations to do just that.

This is happening all over the world today, and not only in poor nations. In the United States the specter of the loss of capital investment has increasingly been used as a threat to keep unions cooperative and to make both federal and local agencies more reluctant to impose environmental and safety regulations. Some think that real wages in the United States have declined overall since the early 1970s, especially for the middle class.[4] According to Ricardo, as long as capital moves freely across national boundaries, wages will decline until they are on the same level as those of all the other nations with which we trade freely.[5]

Ricardo could dismiss these implications of free trade because in his day capital did not move freely across national boundaries:

> Experience, however, shows that the fancied or real insecurity of capital, when not under the immediate control of its owner, together with the natural disinclination which every man has to quit the country of his birth and connections, and intrust himself, with all his habits fixed, to a strange government and new laws, check the emigration of capital. These feelings, which I should be sorry to see weakened, induce most men of property to be satisfied with a low rate of profits in their own country, rather than seek a more advantageous employment for their wealth in foreign nations.[6]

Because of this "natural disinclination" to move capital, Ricardo could use the theory of comparative advantage to argue for free trade. Today no such "disinclination" stops the movement of capital, and thus the consequences of free trade are very different. But economists look at trade through the narrow view provided by the theory of comparative advantage as removed from its original context and enshrined in deductive theory. Consequently they continue to argue for free trade with virtually no consideration of the changed circumstance of the movement of capital. Economists for the most part no longer read Ricardo's original argument; they learn only the conclusions of it—and often through a later formulation by someone else—in complete abstraction from the particular historical circumstances in which it was formed and upon which its conclusions depend. Consequently in the debate about free trade versus protectionism the full implications of the free movement of capital and labor are simply not considered.

The idea that free trade is mutually beneficial because of the principle of comparative advantage was retained, but Ricardo's further assertion that the effectiveness of comparative advantage depends on capital and labor not moving freely across national boundaries was forgotten. For over a hundred years that circumstance could be taken for granted. And in the intensely efficient focus of deductive method, what can be taken for granted simply disappears from sight: it is unnecessary and inefficient to keep stipulating the obvious. The problem of deductive method is precisely this tendency so to abstract the theory from the historical circumstances that when the circumstances change in a crucial respect, no one even realizes the theory needs to be adjusted.

But the choice for deductive method did not go unchallenged. Thomas Malthus was worried about the consequences of the quest for clarity at all costs:

> The principal cause of error, and of the differences which prevail at present among the scientific writers on political economy, appears to me to be a precipitate attempt to simplify and generalize.

In political economy the desire to simplify has occasioned an unwillingness to acknowledge the operation of more causes than one in the production of particular effects; and if one cause would account for a considerable portion of a certain class of phenomena, the whole has been ascribed to it without sufficient attention to the facts, which would not admit of being so solved.

It is certain that we cannot too highly respect and venerate that admirable rule of Newton, not to admit more causes than are necessary to the solution of the phenomena we are considering; but the rule itself implies, that those which really are necessary must be admitted.[7]

Unfortunately, but understandably, Malthus's cautions went largely unheeded. In the murky world of economic life, where questions of economics could have life-and-death implications for starving people, clarity that could promise some capacity to control economic forces was desperately needed and gratefully accepted.

Malthus was often shown to be wrong in his economic analysis, and Ricardo right; thus Ricardo's use of deductive method was thought to be brilliantly vindicated, and Malthus's warnings about oversimplifying and overgeneralizing were ignored. Only in the twentieth century, when John Maynard Keynes adjusted neoclassical theory to take account of some important dimensions to which the theory had been blind, was Malthus shown to be right on some key issues, such as the role that encouraging consumption can play.

The fact that Malthus was seen as identifying with the interests of the landlord class and opposing those of the laboring class did not help. Not only Marx, but Malthus's own utilitarians disagreed with his conservatism.[8] Once again, the politics of the situation affected the focus and outcome of the theoretical discussion. The theoretical problem was the nature and causes of "rent" and the role of the land in contributing to exchange value. The political problem was that British landlords were protected by the Corn Laws, which placed heavy tariffs on the import of "corn" (staple grains such as wheat), keeping corn prices high. High corn prices meant that manufacturers had to pay more to laborers to maintain them at a subsistence level. So both capital and labor lost out to the landlords, who reaped the benefit of high food prices through the rent paid to them by tenant farmers.

Ricardo, with his deductive style, accepted the division of the factors of production among "land," "labor," and "capital" and decided to focus on the question of distribution: how are the fruits of production distributed among landlords, laborers, and capitalists?

The produce of the earth—all that is derived from its surface by the united application of labor, machinery, and capital, is divided among three classes of the community, namely, the proprietor of the land, the owner of the stock or capital necessary for its cultivation, and the laborers by whose industry it is cultivated. "To determine the laws which regulate this distribution is the principal problem in Political Economy."9

Thus we see on the first page of Ricardo's *Principles* that his focus will be much narrower than that of Adam Smith, who thought that the principal problem in economics was to figure out broadly how to encourage the growth of national wealth. Though Ricardo no less than Smith wanted to encourage economic growth, he was more interested in methodology and paid much less attention to wider issues.

Malthus, by contrast, begins his *Principles* with a discussion of the contribution of Adam Smith, the complexity of the subject, and the importance of attention to actual circumstances:

> The first business of philosophy is to account for things as they are; and till our theories will do this, they ought not to be the ground of any practical conclusion. . . . A theory may appear to be correct, and may really be correct under given premises; it may further appear that these premises are the same as those under which the theory is about to be applied; but a difference which might before have been unobserved, may shew itself . . . ; and the theory may justly be considered as failing.10

Although Ricardo defined economics in terms of a particular problem on which he focused—distribution—Malthus, like Smith, was more interested in broader questions and more sensitive to their complexities. It is no wonder, then, that Ricardo was more successful, but part of the price paid was ultimately the loss of "land" as an important and unique factor of production. Another ultimate cost was the loss of any serious critique of the basic assumptions and tenets of economic theory in light of changing historical circumstances and changing knowledge about human nature.

This difference in fundamental focus and method between Ricardo and Malthus led to much misunderstanding between them on the issue of the Corn Laws and the role of rent. The misunderstanding is important because it lent support to the denial of the importance of land as a unique factor of production in both Marxian and classical economics. We might say that Ricardo looked at rent as a distribution problem that depended on the politics of supply and demand, and Malthus looked at rent as a problem of production that depended on the contribution to supply made by the produce of the land.

Ricardo looked at the high price of corn in England and asked why it was high. His answer was that the interaction of demand and supply made it high. Supply was limited by the Corn Laws, which kept out cheap imported corn, and by the problem of diminishing returns in agriculture. Everyone knew that as the population grew, demand for corn grew, but there were limits on how much could be grown on English farms. More labor applied to fertile land eventually reached the point of diminishing returns, and even more labor applied to marginal land did the same, only sooner. One might think this situation would prompt economists to consider the importance of natural limits, and thus the unique nature of the land and the contribution of absolute scarcity of land and resources (not just relative scarcity) to exchange value. But Ricardo's theoretical framework combined powerfully with the political situation to keep this dimension of the problem from view.

Exchange value, according to Ricardo's theory, depends almost entirely on the amount of labor embodied in the product, and not at all on the amount or quality of the resources used to make up the product.[11] As we saw in Adam Smith's work, this was accepted because land and resources were thought of as "free" to all, costing only the "toil and trouble" of appropriating them. This theory was not based entirely on the common myths about what was true for humankind "in a state of nature." In Britain the "common lands" had existed for centuries and had been free to everyone to use for such basics of subsistence as fuel, game for the table, and pasturage for a milk cow and a few sheep.[12] Before the invasion of William the Conqueror, much of the land was held in common. But feudalization imposed a system of overlords who were given legal title to the land that had been common. The "common lands" became smaller and smaller, and population growth added to the pressure, yet people still continued to obtain subsistence livings from them. When the factory system was arising, it was common for industrialists to complain that the people would rather live in poverty off the land than earn a wage in a factory. British historian Christopher Hill notes "numerous seventeenth-century references to the English national characteristic of hating labour more than death." For example,

> Tawney emphasized the contrast between having the status of wage-labourer thrust upon one and being able to choose between that and working on the land as a squatter. "The former is slavery; the latter is freedom."[13]

I suspect that this option of being able to earn a subsistence living from the common lands was sufficiently real that Adam Smith was able to assume that participation in the market was voluntary: If laborers did not like the wages offered, they could, quite literally, go fishing, or live off the land in some other way. This hypothesis of voluntary participation was accepted as a key element of economic theory and remains basic in today's neoclassical framework. Voluntary participation is an essential condition for the equitable and efficient operation of a free market. But many economists and policy makers have confused the requirement for an actuality, frequently asserting that participation in free markets is in fact voluntary. Once again, the historical condition, which made subsistence from the land a real option, was taken for granted; the hypothesis of voluntary participation was set into the theory and abstracted from the condition; the actual situation changed as access to the means of subsistence living disappeared, but the theory was not revised.

This was true in Ricardo's time, even though the appropriation of the land by the lords was deeply resented and formed part of the politics of the controversy over the Corn Laws and the pressure for free trade. To return to the problem of rent and of exchange value, Ricardo states the question this way:

> It remains however to be considered whether the appropriation of land, and the consequent creation of rent, will occasion any variation in the relative value of commodities independently of the quantity of labour necessary to production.[14]

Ricardo accepts Smith's contention that rent "is that portion of the produce of the earth which is paid to the landlord for the use of the original and indestructible powers of the soil."[15] However, the practice of paying rent does not arise because of those powers and the importance of maintaining them. On the contrary, where land is abundant and fertile, one would no sooner rent land than one would rent air and water. Rent, then, arises only when land is appropriated from general use by a few and made scarce either by that appropriation or by population pressure. This scarcity of supply in relation to the demand means that more labor will be employed to get more food from less fertile land, because the higher price of corn will make it possible for farmers to pay the extra labor. Ricardo concludes that "rent invariably proceeds from the employment of an additional quantity of labour with a proportionally less return."[16]

This means that it is the cost of labor, not the amount of rent, that affects the cost of grain:

> The reason, then, why raw produce rises in comparative value is because more labour is employed in the production of the last portion obtained, and not because a rent is paid to the landlord.[17]

The necessity of putting more labor into food production in order to meet the demand for grain causes the supply price of grain to rise. According to Ricardo, rent occurred only because the landlords were able to force labor and capital to give up some of their share in order to gain access to the land.

Now we see why landlords were so resented, and why businesspeople sought to escape their power by repealing the Corn Laws and trading for cheaper grain abroad. The way Ricardo framed the discussion, using the emphasis on distribution and the already accepted labor theory of value, led to the focus on the competition among landlords, laborers, and capitalists for the fruits of production. In this one instance at least, labor and capital were at one—against the landlords. Ricardo seemed to prove that rent had nothing to do with "the productive powers of the soil" and everything to do with unjust appropriation of those powers.

Scarcity as a problem of natural limits inherent in the land rather than as a political issue did not trouble Ricardo. If his labor theory of value was right, then scarcity was automatically covered by the cost of applying more labor to get the same return. Ricardo's horizon was bounded by the economic problems of England. If rising population pushed the farmland in England to the limit, then the Corn Laws must be repealed and corn imported from the almost limitless land of North America. The idea that a time might come when there was no further land available, and no amount of further application of labor and capital could increase the food supply, or the resources (such as wood) available for industrial production, any further, seems not to have been considered by Ricardo. He understands that "everything rises or falls in value in proportion to the facility or difficulty of producing it."[18] But this is the same thing, he immediately adds, as "in proportion to the quantity of labour employed on its production."

While contemporary neoclassical economists no longer accept Ricardo's assessment of rent and do not hold the labor theory of value, in important respects the theory still functions as if they did. Efficiency is still primarily measured in terms of labor productivity. In agriculture this means that the more capital- and energy-intensive the method, the more "productive" it is— because less labor is needed—regardless of the consequences, which include the gradual loss of "the productive powers of the soil" by largely irreversible abuse of the land. Marxian economists do still accept the labor theory of value, as we shall see.

Ricardo was right about the cause of rent in the historical circumstances in which he considered it. Rent does not arise in conditions of abundance and free access. And an abundance of fertile land lowers exchange value rather than adding to it. He correctly observed that French economist J. B. Say continually confused value in use with value in exchange, concluding mistakenly that the produce of an abundance of fertile land and resources adds to exchange value. The produce adds greatly to "riches," which depend on use value, but not to exchange value, because an abundant supply always means a lower price:

> M. Say accuses Dr. Smith of having overlooked the value which is given to commodities by natural agents, and by machinery, because he considered that the value of all things was derived from the labour of man; but it does not appear to me that this charge is made out; for Adam Smith nowhere undervalues the services which these natural agents and machinery perform for us, but he very justly distinguishes the nature of the value which they add to commodities—they are serviceable to us, by

increasing the abundance of productions, by making men richer, by adding to value in use; but as they perform their work gratuitously, as nothing is paid for the use of air, of heat, and of water, the assistance which they afford us adds nothing to value in exchange.[19]

What Ricardo did not have before him to consider was the situation in which scarcity was caused neither by monopolistic appropriation nor by trade barriers, but by absolute scarcity relative to demand. In this case, all the extra labor in the world could not increase the supply. Ricardo was aware that this sort of thing might happen. He discusses the situation in which one person gains control of water, remarking that while this enriches the one, everyone else is impoverished. A monopoly changes the distribution, not the supply, of water. However,

> If it should be scarce, then the riches of the country and of individuals would be actually diminished, inasmuch as it would be deprived of a portion of its enjoyments. . . . Not only would there be a different distribution of riches, but an actual loss of wealth.[20]

While recognizing that absolute scarcity of an essential resource is possible, Ricardo does not seem interested in considering any implications this would have for his labor theory of value. Would not the exchange value of water rise, when the same amount of labor was required to appropriate the smaller amounts now available? In the next paragraph he goes on to say:

> It may be said, then, of two countries possessing precisely the same quantity of all the necessaries and comforts of life, that they are equally rich, but the value of their respective riches would depend on the comparative facility or difficulty with which they were produced.

Though this statement is true, it focuses on comparing exchange values when the two countries "are equally rich" and blindly accepts the theoretical assertion that the difference of exchange value is caused entirely by different labor input.

Why this lack of interest in the question that the problem of absolute scarcity raises for value theory? First, it was not because it seemed a remote problem of little pressing concern. Technological innovation was continually overcoming the bottlenecks of production and introducing substitutes for scarce resources. Ricardo does take note of this, but this source of hope did not have the status that it has grown to have in our era.[21] Ricardo, like all the classical economists, agreed with Thomas Malthus that population always expands more rapidly than food resources, and that eventually the world would be faced with a situation in which food production could not be expanded further, and only starvation could regulate population growth. This was known as the hypothesis of the "stationary state." One might think that this acknowledgment of natural limits would occasion some theoretical reflection on the labor theory of value, but that was not the case.

Instead, Ricardo seems to have believed that the "stationary state" of the economy would be reached long before the situation of absolute scarcity was reached. This would happen because of the natural tendency of the rate of profit to fall:

> For, in the progress of society and wealth, the additional quantity of food required is obtained by the sacrifice of more and more labour. . . . The rise in the price of necessaries and in the wages of labour is, however, limited; for as soon as wages should be equal . . . to . . . the whole receipts of the farmer, there must be an end to [capital] accumulation; for no capital can then yield any profit whatever, and no additional labour can be demanded, and consequently population will have reached its highest point. Long, indeed, before this period, the very low rate of profits will have arrested all accumulation. . . .
>
> Thus we again arrive at the same conclusion which we have before attempted to establish:—that in all countries, and all times, profits depend on the quantity of labour requisite to provide necessaries for the labourers on that land or with that capital which yields no rent. The effects then of accumulation [of capital] will be different in different countries, and will depend chiefly on the fertility of the land.[22]

Ricardo seems to be arguing that long before wages equal return, capitalists will simply stop investing, and production will grind to a halt until it is once more possible for sufficient profit to be made to attract investors. He does not describe how this would come about, but as he insists that profits depend on wages being low enough, clearly wages would have to fall. Because in Ricardo's view wages are already at subsistence levels, the only way wages could fall would be for the population to drop until the amount of labor required to produce enough food dropped far enough for the price of food to go down. Presumably, if each laborer had fewer children, "subsistence" for fewer children per laborer would be less, and wages would drop. But Ricardo does not address the problem of how to achieve a sustainably small population in relation to food production.

Ricardo, then, seems to assume that the problem of absolute scarcity (as for example the scarcity of fertile land) is "covered" by the labor theory of value. Every time he seems on the verge of admitting that absolute scarcity plays a role in exchange value independent of labor, he reasserts that the exchange value is not only measured but determined by the cost of labor.[23]

Ricardo does think that capital and land contribute to wealth, but land, at least, does not contribute to exchange value, so he has no room for a concept of absolute scarcity in his views of exchange value. Ricardo approvingly quotes a French contemporary on this:

> This also, I am happy to say, appears to be M. Destutt de Tracy's opinion.[24] He says, "As it is certain that our physical and moral faculties are alone our original riches, the employment of those faculties, labour of some kind, is our only original treasure, and that it is always from this employment that all those things are created which we call riches, those which are the most necessary as well as those which are the most purely agreeable. It is certain too, that all those things only represent the labour which has created them, and if they have a value, or even two distinct values, they can only derive them from that of the labour from which they emanate."[25]

This view that labor creates exchange value and most of use value is based on a concept of "absolute natural abundance." It is similar to Adam Smith's view that the bottleneck to greater production was the productivity of labor, not any absolute scarcity of land and resources.

Although Ricardo and Smith were right about the bottleneck of their day, when they moved to theoretical generalization they might have been more careful to allow for the role that absolute limits could play in the future. They were well aware that land and resources such as metals are fixed for the earth as a whole. Thomas Malthus did think that absolute scarcity was an important issue, but he was not able to articulate its implications in a way that increased theoretical clarity in value theory and the argument over rent.

Malthus insists that land is a unique factor of production and this uniqueness makes possible the payment of rent. He bases his argument on the fact that land is the only source of food, which is essential to maintain human life. When farm laborers can produce only enough food to feed themselves, with no surplus, then no labor can be given to manufacturing and trade, and no rent can be paid.[26]

Ricardo similarly says that farms operating at the margin of food production can afford no rent, though they will pay profits to the investor, or the land would not have been used. Typical of the confusions in their economic discussions is this situation in which Malthus is thinking of subsistence farming while Ricardo is evidently considering only farming for the market. But Malthus goes on to claim that it is therefore the fertility of land—its capacity to support labor beyond subsistence—that makes rent possible. Ricardo claims that fertility does not give rise to rent, scarcity does. From here the argument goes around and around. Again, confusion.

Yet at this stage both are right. Malthus is right that fertility makes the payment of rent possible, and Ricardo is right that it is scarcity that makes the payment of rent necessary. Ricardo means relative scarcity due to appropriation and to trade barriers, and clearly distinguishes between marginal land for which no rent can be charged and fertile land that reaps rent because the price depends on the cost of using the marginal land, which of course is higher than for fertile land. But Malthus wrongly concludes that fertility is the cause of rent:

> If no rent can exist without this surplus, and if the power of particular soils to pay rent be proportioned to this surplus, it follows that this surplus from the land, arising from its fertility, must evidently be considered as the foundation or main cause of all rent.[27]

We may achieve some clarity by saying that Malthus is right that surplus produce is the foundation of rent (because without it rent cannot be paid), but wrong about it being the cause of rent, while Ricardo is right that scarcity is the cause, since without scarcity rent cannot be exacted.

The whole argument is important because of the consequences for how economics has treated land since then. Malthus was well aware that Ricardo was basing his argument about rent on a condition of original abundance of land:

> It is so obviously true, as to be hardly worth stating, that if the land of the greatest fertility were in such excessive plenty compared with the population, that every man might help himself to as much as he wanted, there would be no rents or landlords so called.[28]

But, says Malthus, this is no part of the reality of the world today, and "it is of no sort of use to dwell upon, and draw general inferences from suppositions which never can take place."[29] Malthus accepts the necessity of landlords for the ensuring of a food supply and is more interested in this role of the land in enabling the growth of wealth in a nation than he was in Ricardo's focus on distribution. Ricardo wanted to attain clarity about exchange value, while Malthus wanted to understand wealth (in the sense of Smith's actual "necessaries and conveniencies of life").

Unfortunately, not only was Malthus less clear than Ricardo on rent, he was wrong about its causes. This cast a shadow over his consequent policy recommendations and over his further theoretical conclusions. For our purposes, the most important of these was his discussion of the contribution of the land to wealth and value. Malthus was convinced, like the Physiocrats, Smith, and Say, that land has unique importance for economics:

> It is . . . strictly true, that land produces the necessaries of life—produces the means by which, and by which alone, an increase of people may be brought into being and supported. In this respect it is fundamentally different from every other kind of ma-

chine known to man; and it is natural to suppose that the use of it should be attended with some peculiar effects.³⁰

An example Malthus gives of one of these "peculiar" effects of the land is a supposition about a farm family: If they can produce enough food for themselves and five extra laborers, they can use the extra labor to produce all sorts of other goods. But if they can produce only enough food for themselves and also have a machine for making hats for fifty people, the machine does them no good because they have no surplus labor to use for it, and no guarantee of a market for the hats.³¹ All the capital in the world, then, is no substitute for sufficient produce from the land.

This recognition of a unique role for land in the production of wealth gives a different flavor to the economic discussion than Ricardo's focus on the role of labor to the exclusion of land. Like Ricardo, Malthus recognized the distinction between wealth and exchange value, and is careful in his discussion of value to distinguish them, but with this distinctive view of land:

> Unquestionably the American labourer is richer, and much better off than the English labourer. He obtains the command of a quantity of food more than sufficient to maintain his largest family; . . . But he evidently does not purchase what he obtains by a greater sacrifice than the English labourer. He does not give more for what he receives, but receives more for what he gives. . . . We must make the proper distinction between value and riches, and say that he is rich, not because he possesses a greater value to give in exchange for what he wants, but because what he wants, or the main articles which constitute this riches, are obtained with much more facility, and are really more abundant and cheaper than they are in Europe.³²

The American laborer is richer than the English laborer, according to Malthus, not because labor and capital are more productive in America than in England. If anything, the techniques used with labor and capital were probably less efficient in America. In the modern sense of productivity, we probably would say that labor and capital are more productive, but only because we do not acknowledge the crucial contribution in this case of the superior abundance of the third factor—land. It would be more accurate to say that the economy of America was more productive than that of England because the abundance of land and natural resources outweighed the relative inefficiency of labor and capital. While Malthus agrees with Ricardo that the "labour worked up in a commodity is the principal cause of its value," he goes on to argue that this is not the way to measure value, because other factors make a contribution that is reflected in how much labor a commodity can "command."³³

To go into more detail about Malthus's "labor command" theory of value versus Ricardo's labor theory of value would serve no clear purpose. We have already seen that Malthus wants to include the unique contribution of the land in a way that Ricardo does not. Ricardo not only accepted the choice of labor as the most convenient way to measure exchange value but also thought of labor as the cause of exchange value. Malthus, more interested in wealth, insisted on the unique contribution of land to production, but he was unable to articulate clearly the circumstances in which land also contributes to exchange value— namely, those of absolute scarcity in which the increase of labor can no longer increase or even maintain the supply of particular resources from that land.

This argument between Ricardo and Malthus about rent and value illustrates two fundamental tendencies of all subsequent economic theory, including Marxian. The first is the tendency to focus on the roles of labor and capital to the exclusion of the unique contribution of the land in the production of wealth. The second is the tendency to ignore or deny any need to consider the conditions in which land and resources play a role in exchange value, and how that role might also be unique. Both tendencies were reinforced by the intense desire to avoid the specter of the subsistence "stationary state."

As mentioned above, the "stationary state" was thought to be the eventual, inevitable outcome of economic growth, when the limits of food supply and production would be reached. Malthus, in *An Essay on the Principle of Population, as It Affects the Future Improvement of Society*, first published in 1798, argues that every improvement in wages and food supply will call forth a larger labor force. Since population grows geometrically, and agricultural output can improve only arithmetically—with diminishing returns—eventually population will outstrip the food supply. This led to the argument that high wages will only encourage laborers to have many more children, who will grow up to place more demands on agriculture than can be met, which will lead to greater poverty in the end. The inescapable conclusion seemed to be that it is unwise to pay labor more than subsistence wages, and worse yet to grant "poor relief."[34] This is how Malthus earned for economics the name "the dismal science," while he earned for himself the hatred of champions of the working class— especially Marx.[35]

The idea of a "stationary state" for the economy became for economists and policy makers a nightmare vision of the whole world as a teeming slum of barely subsisting laborers pressing against the food supply—what we see today in nations like Bangladesh. It quickly became apparent that the only way to hold off the nightmare, and at the same time to improve the situation of laborers, was through technical innovation. By constantly improving the productivity of labor by means of invention and increases in capital stock, and constantly enlarging the food supply through new sources of food (which for England meant abolition of the Corn Laws and free trade in food, secured especially by colonization) and new means of getting more food from the land, the specter of the stationary state could be held off. In just a few decades economics moved from the discovery that economic growth is possible to the conviction that growth is necessary to stave off disaster.

In the next century and a half, the cautions of Malthus about population growth and resource limits were not heeded. Instead of leading economists to consider the importance of the land, the maintenance of its fertility, and the frugal use of its resources, the specter of the stationary state instead led to a search for ways to stave it off that centered on economic growth. Instead of searching for ways to develop the economy within the constraints of nature, every effort was made to escape from them. Technical innovation and economic growth were so successful.at this that within a few decades economists and policy makers had developed an unshakable faith in their ability to overcome all limits in the long run. There was ample evidence for this faith. In the course of over one hundred years every obstacle was overcome. When whale oil became scarce, petroleum was discovered and harnessed. When American farms began to lose their virginal fertility, chemical fertilizers were developed, and the productivity of the land soared—until very recently. It is not surprising, then, that this faith in technical innovation and economic growth has become a central tenet of popular culture in the United States and is one area that few economists and politicians question.

3

For Maximizing Wealth with Social Redistribution over Production Reform: John Stuart Mill

JOHN STUART MILL (1806–1873) can almost be discussed as two different economists. On the one hand, his theoretical work continued and refined that of David Ricardo. His 1836 essay "On the Definition of Political Economy and the Method of Investigation Proper to It" is a classic still studied for its clarifying discussion of deductive method. On the other hand, when he comes to discuss concrete economic problems in his 1848 *Principles of Political Economy*, he does not allow his previous theoretical principles to interfere with his observations. With Mill's Principles we broaden out again from the narrow focus of David Ricardo and return to the wide-ranging scope first shown by Adam Smith. Like Smith, Mill is interested in everything, and like Smith, he does not systematize his richly complex discussion according to theoretical considerations—at least not according to his own highly abstract deductive method. Consequently, Mill provides us with a view of economics that contains several important contributions yet to be fully realized. At the same time, it is perhaps a blessing that he did not systematize his work, since theoretical considerations might have led him to drop the very material that from our perspective is of most interest.

Mill the pure theorist gave us the concept of *Homo economicus*, "man" as the self-interested wealth maximizer, and he defended eloquently the use of deductive method. His theory therefore reinforced the prior choices for individualism and growth. Yet Mill the political economist gave us an insightful discussion of what makes for healthy agriculture, and even discussed nature, the land, and absolute scarcity in terms not heard before—terms with real potential for correcting the loss of land as a unique factor in economics. Perhaps the key to these two Mills is that he simply did not see any tension between theoretical individualism and actual economic communities. Mill was an optimist, an heir of the Enlightenment faith in education and reason. He was convinced that society would eventually be able to work out the inequality of wealth that marred capitalist industrialization by means of distribution mechanisms and birth control.

It is for these ideas about distribution that Mill is best remembered. Unlike Marx, who attacked capitalism in terms of who benefited from production, Mill accepted the productive processes and the shares of wages, profit, and rent as part of the "laws of production." But he believed that these processes did not preclude the redistribution of the fruits of production through social programs of taxation, welfare, and the like. At a stroke Mill split the liberal tradition into two streams, and transformed the stationary state from a specter to a potential utopia. This split in liberalism continues to this day and has very much set the terms of the social debate in the United States.

First, let us consider Mill the theorist. Although it was Ricardo who first used deductive method with telling effect in economics, it was Mill who described deductive economic theory with new clarity. In contrast to Ricardo, who defines political economy in terms of the problem of distribution, Mill asserts that "Political Economy" is concerned with

> man . . . solely as a being who desires to possess wealth, and who is capable of judging of the comparative efficacy of means for obtaining that end. It predicts only such of the phenomena of the social state as take place in consequence of the pursuit of wealth. It makes entire abstraction of every other human passion or motive; except those which may be regarded as perpetually antagonizing principles to the desire of wealth, namely, aversion to labour, and desire of the present enjoyment of costly indulgences.[1]

As described thus far, the theory would seem to be entirely neutral. Political economy is attempting simply to describe the behavior of people insofar as they act with the motive of gaining wealth. But even with this first step, Mill has chosen to define economics in terms narrowly restricted to one motive and one outcome—the desire for wealth. This is a crucial value choice for economics, because it restricts attention to behavior directed to achieving this one value. Other motives for economic activity, such as achieving a healthy level of community subsistence, engaging in types of work that are more satisfying because more interesting and more personal, working with others to build something needed, such as housing: all these motives are defined as outside the concern of economics.

While it is true that some economic theorists, many decades later, did realize the difficulty of stipulating "the pursuit of wealth" as the foundational motive for economic behavior, their clarification of the issue (discussed in chapter 5) did not occur in time to change the impact of Mill's definition on decades of economists. Nor does it seem unwarranted to assert that in American culture economics has come to be understood very much in terms of this narrow focus, and is still so understood. Mill's act of wedding Ricardo's deductive method with Smith's choices for growth and individualism proved effective in both the theory and in the popular culture.

It is often argued that the "wealth-maximizing" motive, as it came to be called, was chosen because it is obviously the most powerful motive in human behavior. The beauty of capitalism, goes the argument, is precisely in being able to harness this motive to achieve economic growth. No one denies this. The question is, was wealth maximizing already naturally the most powerful human motive, or was it focused on and cultivated assiduously for two hundred years, until today we cannot imagine it as anything but natural? If wealth maximizing really is the most powerful natural human motive, how was it possible for thousands of years of human existence, in very diverse cultures and historical epochs, to keep it from dominating human behavior? This is a complex issue to which I cannot do justice—about which, indeed, we may not have enough evidence to draw conclusions. Human beings were certainly subject to the desire for riches long before the industrial era. However, it is important to recognize that economic theory, far from being neutrally descriptive, accepted and encouraged both the social choice of the modern era for economic growth and the choice to focus on and cultivate the wealth-maximizing motive as the most efficient means for achieving the goal of growth.

Indeed, economics not only accepted these two value choices but also encouraged them. In the case of Mill, immediately after he describes economics as interested in a human being solely as one who is interested in gaining wealth, he adds that political economy

> aims at showing what is the course of action into which mankind, living in a state of society, would be impelled, if that motive, except in the degree in which it is checked by the two perpetual counter-motives above adverted to [aversion to labor and desire to enjoy luxuries], were absolute ruler of all their actions.[2]

Insofar as economics really has tended to concentrate on how to realize fully the motive of gaining wealth, as if it were the only motive, economics has gone much further than a neutral discussion of economic behavior. Mill has opted here to reinforce Adam Smith's choices for the growth of the production of wealth as the central aim of economics and to cultivate the individual desire for wealth as the most efficient way to achieve growth.

Even more important than Mill's acceptance of economic gain as the goal of economic theory is this placement of the individual desire for wealth, abstracted from any other motive, as the central thesis around which all else must revolve. Mill justifies this sharp focus on the grounds that science must isolate the most important phenomena and ignore the rest to be effective. Consequently a priori reasoning is necessary in economics:

> [Political economy] reasons, and, as we contend, must necessarily reason, from assumptions, not from facts. It is built upon hypotheses strictly analogous to those which, under the name of definitions, are the foundation of the other abstract sciences. Geometry presupposes an arbitrary definition of a line, "that which has length but not breadth." Just in the same manner does Political Economy presuppose an arbitrary definition of man, as a being who invariably does that by which he may obtain the greatest amount of necessaries, conveniences, and luxuries, with the smallest quantity of labour and physical self-denial with which they can be obtained in the existing state of knowledge. . . .
>
> The conclusions of geometry are not strictly true of such lines, angles, and figures, as human hands can construct. But no one, therefore, contends that the conclusions of geometry are of no utility, or that it would be better to shut up Euclid's Elements, and content ourselves with "practice" and "experience."[3]

This description of "man" as a wealth maximizer (which came to be called *Homo economicus*), compared to the mathematical abstraction of a line, is telling. Human hands in Western culture are continually striving in their constructions to achieve more and more exact approximations to mathematically perfect "lines, angles, and figures." Probably no other culture in history has been so intent on standardizing and perfecting its modes of measurement—down to the width of atoms.

To liken *Homo economicus* to the mathematical line is to set up the image as an ideal to be actualized more and more perfectly in economic behavior, just as the line is an ideal to be actualized in building construction. The implications of what Mill has done go far beyond simply abstracting for purposes of theoretical clarity. He has constructed an economic model that enshrines wealth-maximizing behavior as fundamental and normative, in isolation from all other social considerations. I would contend that Western culture has gradually come to actualize that model more and more, until economic behavior is commonly understood to be about wealth maximizing, and it is in fact conducted more and more in isolation from all other dimensions of life. Further, since so much time is spent in economic behavior, life itself is more and more dominated by this concern for wealth maximizing. We have very much remade human societies so that people work and live in different places; they live in isolated nuclear families in isolating suburban houses; their work is completely disconnected from any awareness of the natural world, from relationship with their children, or from any relationship with the consequences of their work.

While John Stuart Mill did not cause this long-term cultural trend, the assumptions of his deductive theory certainly illustrate the social movement in that direction, and may have abetted it.

The extent to which this choice to encourage "wealth-maximizing" behavior can be termed good or bad is not yet at issue here. The point is that the choice was made. Even though economists did eventually "clean up" the theory by changing "wealth-maximizing" to "utility-maximizing" (which leaves it to individuals to decide what values to maximize), the reality is that "wealth-maximizing" behavior became a powerful dimension not only of Western economics but of Western culture, and is being exported around the world. Utility maximizing, in practice, too often really means wealth maximizing.

John Stuart Mill himself, however, would probably be appalled to know the extent to which human beings have come to resemble *Homo economicus*—a being isolated from the natural world, whose life is splintered, with no connections between its various parts and often with conflicting value systems functioning in the different spheres. Mill seems not to have foreseen any such results for deductive theory. By contrast, Mill's *Principles of Political Economy*, which was published twelve years after his essay on theory, gives us a much richer, more complex, and more realistic view of the world.

Especially interesting for our purposes is Mill's understanding of land and nature. Early economic thinker William Petty described nature as the passive "mother" and labor as the active "father" of economic production. In contrast to Petty and to much of Western philosophy, Mill really understood the role of nature in economics to be active, not passive:

> Cases like this, in which a certain amount of labour has been dispensed with, its work being devolved upon some natural agent, are apt to suggest an erroneous notion of the comparative functions of labour and natural powers; as if the co-operation of those powers with human industry were limited to the cases in which they are made to perform what would otherwise be done by labour; as if, in the case of things made (as the phrase is) by hand, nature only furnished passive materials. This is an illusion. The powers of nature are as actively operative in the one case as in the other. . . . This one operation, of putting things into fit places for being acted upon by their own internal forces, and by those residing in other natural objects, is all that man does, or can do, with matter. He only moves one thing to or from another. He moves a seed into the ground; and the natural forces of vegetation produce in succession a root, a stem, leaves, flowers, and fruit. He moves an axe through a tree, and it falls by the natural force of gravitation. . . . He moves a spark to fuel, and it ignites, and by the force generated in combustion it cooks the food, melts or softens the iron, converts into beer or sugar the malt or cane-juice, which he has previously moved to the spot. He has no other means of acting on matter than by moving it. . . .
>
> Labour, then, in the physical world, is always and solely employed in putting ob-

jects in motion; the properties of matter, the laws of nature, do the rest. The skill and ingenuity of human beings are chiefly exercised in discovering movements, practicable by their powers, and capable of bringing about the effects which they desire.4

With this image of nature as the main actor and labor as no more than a participant, Mill gives us a genuine reversal of the image of nature that has been dominant in modern Western civilization. The importance of this reversal for every area of our culture can hardly be exaggerated. Many fundamental images of Western culture would have to be revised—from the psychology that defines women as passive, to the theological tradition that denigrates nature, to the enthusiastic attempt of Western civilization to conquer and control the whole planet—should we accept this reversal. Potentially, then, Mill is here indicating some foundations for a very different worldview, and consequently for a very different economics.

We do indeed find much more sensitivity to the inherent uniqueness of the land throughout Mill's economics. Early in the *Principles,* under "Requisites of Production," Mill asserts that of primary importance is a distinction between "practically unlimited" and "limited" powers.5 The chief of these latter is fertile land. Mill also discusses water, natural resources (such as coal), and fisheries as natural sources which can become limited and thus bear a market price. At this stage Mill does not mention the role of labor but rather seems to intimate that the exchange value realized by scarcity of land and resources appears in rent.

Later in the book Mill returns to the topic of the land. He is concerned to point out that, even though everyone knows land to be the ultimate limit, the fact is that the limits of the land have never been reached, so it is commonly thought that it will be ages before they will be reached. Mill claims that this is "not only an error, but the most serious one, to be found in the whole field of political economy."6 Further, Mill emphatically asserts that this question

> is more important and fundamental than any other; it involves the whole subject of the causes of poverty, in a rich and industrious community: and unless this one matter be thoroughly understood, it is to no purpose proceeding any further in our inquiry.7

Mill is referring to the law of diminishing returns in agriculture, whereby "the very meaning of inferior land, is land which with equal labour returns a smaller amount of produce."8 Mill puts the matter very differently than Ricardo, who thought of inferior land as land that required more labor to produce the same amount of food. Ricardo thought that the difference could be made up by more labor and measured in labor costs. Mill, however, kept the focus firmly on the land itself, and not only the labor used on it, which leaves room for understanding that land has limits that no amount of labor can overcome.

(Unfortunately, as far as I know, this difference has never been worked out in economic analysis and formulae. I know of no analytical specifications of absolute scarcity.)

This consistent inclusion of the land in Mill's *Principles* can be noted both in his discussion of concrete economies and in his further theoretical reflections. For example, when he goes on to discuss the ways in which the law of diminishing returns can be mitigated, he never forgets that it can only be mitigated, and not forever avoided, even as he considers in considerable detail the multiple ways that mitigation can be effected—which he puts under the catchall phrase "the progress of civilization." These methods include technological progress and social-cultural changes, practices such as crop rotation, the use of manure, the development of improved tools and methods of their use, improved roads, railways, and canals—and also social changes such as in education and "above all, the acquisition of a permanent interest in the soil by the cultivators of it."9

Leaving aside the theoretical issues for the moment, we see that Mill viewed land as a unique factor in economics and thought it deserved detailed attention. Throughout the *Principles* he never allowed theoretical interests to deflect him from carefully considering such concrete details as how the law of diminishing returns affects the economy—both in agriculture and in manufacturing. Part of this discussion was a wide-ranging consideration of what Mill thought would be healthy social and political practices in relation to these economic problems. When he discusses productivity, he includes the value of widespread education (pages 107–10). When he discusses agriculture, he distinguishes types of agriculture that are part of what he considers to be healthier societies: the "peasant proprietors" of Switzerland have a better agriculture than the landless peasants of France because their small peasant-owned farming system results in a freer, more intelligent, more self-reliant, and more prosperous peasant society. This is certainly a very different economic discussion from that yielded by Ricardo's much narrower use of deductive method. Indeed, Mill much more readily makes these sorts of value judgments than would many successors to his own utilitarian philosophy—those who followed the individualistic and hedonistic elements of utilitarianism to the conclusion that value judgments are solely subjective and individual.

Mill's discussion of what constitutes good agriculture illustrates his focus on the land and his interest in the whole society in relation to the economy (despite his assertion in his earlier essay on economic method that economics abstracts from all except the human pursuit of wealth). It is also highly instructive to anyone contemplating the state of agriculture around the world today. Mill particularly lifts up the "peasant proprietors" of Switzerland as an example of a mode of production that has healthy results for the individual farmers, the land, the community, and the economy as such. He quotes at length from the Swiss economist Jean Sismondi:

> "It is from Switzerland we learn that agriculture practised by the very persons who enjoy its fruits, suffices to procure great comfort for a very numerous population; a great independence of character, arising from independence of position; a great commerce of consumption. . . . , even in a country whose climate is rude, whose land is but moderately fertile . . . all carry in their faces the impress of health and strength. . . .
>
> His little patrimony is a true savings bank, always ready to receive all his little gains. . . . The ever-acting power of nature returns them a hundred-fold. . . .
>
> The peasant proprietor is of all cultivators the one who gets most from the soil, for he is the one who thinks most of the future, and who has been most instructed by experience. He is also the one who employs the human powers to most advantage, because dividing his occupations among all the members of his family, he reserves some for every day of the year, so that nobody is ever out of work. . . . Finally, of all cultivators the peasant proprietor is the one who gives most encouragement to commerce and manufactures, because he is the richest."[10]

Mill goes on to detail the advantages of Swiss agriculture. He notes that much of Swiss prosperity has resulted from the breakup of large feudal estates in which peasants have been allowed to own their own small farms. By comparison, according to Mill, the small farms are much more productive, even compared to "the scientific agriculturist" who farms on a large scale with great capital.[11]

The benefits of peasant-owned small farms are by no means limited to productivity. Mill is very interested in the social-cultural benefits that he sees wherever small farmers own their own land. One of the most important is the self-reliance and intelligence that emerges:

> The mental faculties will be most developed where they are most exercised; and what gives more exercise to them than the having a multitude of interests, none of which can be neglected, and which can be provided for only by varied efforts of will and intelligence? . . . His cares are that he takes his fair share of the business of life; that he is a free human being, and not perpetually a child, which seems to be the approved condition of the labouring classes according to the prevailing philanthropy.[12]

These sentiments were shared by an influential segment of American political thought. Long before Mill, Thomas Jefferson celebrated the importance of a nation of small farmers who could be independent of the control of vested interests in ways that city people could not. Jefferson thought that a democracy depended on widespread ownership of land for its stability. It would be most interesting to study the history of the U.S. Homestead Act of 1862, which deliberately divided frontier land into 160-acre parcels as the size best suited to family farming, which included provision of land for schools, universities, churches, and other community-building institutions, and which forbade the selling of large amounts of land to any one buyer. Although there were "purely economic" reasons for this way of establishing frontier agriculture in the United States, it is clear that the desire to create healthy, self-reliant, and educated communities for the sake of democratic institutions was a factor. It is also clear in the twentieth century that this consideration has given way to what is defined as "economic efficiency," with little debate about the political and social effects of losing to "agribusiness" this original American goal of widespread ownership of land in family farms.

The superiority of Mill's "peasant proprietors," or America's traditional family farmers, to the practices of what Mill calls "the scientific agriculturist" has yet to be debated in terms of social and political benefits, despite studies that demonstrate this.[13] And evidence is mounting for their superiority in safeguarding the long-term health of the land itself.[14] Mill's observation that the small-scale owners of their own land can know more and do more that is adapted to the specific needs of each "little patrimony" is indisputably true, since large-scale capital-intensive farming requires too many acres and too much heavy equipment to allow close attention to the small details and important particularities of each acre of land. Large-scale agribusiness, or "industrial farming," has resulted in such situations as the routine loss of as much as two bushels of Iowa topsoil for each bushel of corn grown.[15] Industrial farming must treat large acreages all alike and cannot be careful of the land to ensure that it remains fertile over generations. Instead, the land is being mined as if we do not expect to need fertile land in the future. While family owned and operated farming on an appropriate scale does not automatically guarantee sustainable farming, as the "Dust Bowl" years taught us, it has been shown to be the easiest, most effective, and proven way to achieve it.

Finally, Mill's assertion that the "peasant proprietor" system is more productive than other types of farming has also gained increasing support—more productive, that is, when measured over a long term, because the fertility of the soil can be maintained much more effectively. Factory farming relies heavily on the substitution of chemical pesticides and fertilizers for the more labor-intensive methods of using manure and other more natural forms of farming. Initially this technique can boost productivity per acre and per labor-hour dramatically. But the gains always eventually fall off, and increasingly we are discovering that these methods actually lead to the permanent destruction of the soil.

The Central Valley of California, for the moment—for a few decades—the most "productive" agricultural region on earth, is being salinized by irrigation. Each year thousands of acres are lost. Before irrigation, traditional small-scale and labor-intensive dry-farming methods could make use of Central Valley land. After salinization, nothing can be grown. Even where irrigation is not practiced, factory farming destroys land with heavy machinery that compacts the soil, chemicals that destroy the complex soil ecology, and monocropping of large acreages, which removes soil cover and windbreaks so that topsoil that took centuries to form blows away in a few years. In order to be economically "efficient," agribusiness must engage in these kinds of factory farming methods. The only kind of farming we know of that can be as labor-intensive as sustainable agriculture needs to be, and yet does not reduce the farmers to abject poverty and dependency, is appropriately scaled family farming. So Mill's observations about agriculture are as relevant today as they were one hundred years before agribusiness really took hold.

Now let us return to the way Mill includes the land and the material source of the economy in his further theoretical reflections. First, there is the distinction Mill draws between "productive" and "unproductive" labor. Mill points out that the word *unproductive* is not meant to imply any stigma, since a great deal of "unproductive" labor—such as that of a surgeon—is both necessary and useful. And productive labor does not mean labor "creative of objects," since "we cannot create matter."[16] Mill agrees with J. B. Say:

> Since, when we are said to produce objects, we only produce utility, why should not all labour which produces utility be accounted productive? Why refuse that title to the surgeon who sets a limb, the judge or legislator who confers security, and give it to the lapidary who cuts and polishes a diamond? Why deny it to the teacher from whom I learn an art by which I can gain my bread, and accord it to the confectioner who makes bonbons for the momentary pleasure of a sense of taste?[17]

The distinction is meant to point to the difference between labor that produces actually usable material and wealth and labor that produces some other sort of utility: "They are all alike in this, that they leave the community richer in material products than they found it; they increase, or tend to increase, material wealth."[18]

Clearly Mill, despite his defense of abstracting deductive method, is interested in the concrete material basis of economic activity. He even claims that money is not and cannot be capital:

> Capital, by persons wholly unused to reflect on the subject, is supposed to be synonymous with money. . . . Money is no more synonymous with capital than it is with wealth. Money cannot in itself perform any part of the office of capital, since it can afford no assistance to production. . . . What capital does for production, is to afford

the shelter, protection, tools and materials which the work requires, and to feed and otherwise maintain the labourers during the process. These are the services which present labour requires from past, and from the produce of past labour.[19]

Though Mill would certainly admit the importance of money as a medium of exchange, he holds steadily to the classical focus on the production of goods as the most important dimension.

It is precisely this focus on production, however, that leads him into his most egregious error: Mill accepts Say's law, which claims that the demand will always be equal to the supply. In other words, there can be no overproduction. Mill thinks that if you have the means of production, you will always be able to do something with what is produced. He remarks that Malthus and others thought that "if consumers were to save and convert into capital more than a limited portion of their income, . . . there would be no market for the commodities which the capital so created would produce."[20] Mill thought this to be "one of the many errors arising in political economy." Mill was wrong, but it was not until John Maynard Keynes solved the puzzle of overproduction in the Great Depression nearly a century later that economics began fully to take into account the role of effective demand. Why was Mill so blind to this problem? The answer is fascinating because it shows how Mill's greatest error is directly connected to his greatest insight. Mill was looking at the problem of effective demand in the terms in which it was understood at the time: "There is not an opinion more general among mankind than this, that the unproductive expenditure of the rich is necessary to the employment of the poor."[21]

It is commonly thought, Mill explains, that if the rich were to save their money from unproductive consumption, demand would drop and the warehouses would fill up with unsold goods. But, he argues, the demand for luxuries for capitalists and landowners would actually fall, while the saved capital would then be used to employ more labor or to pay labor better. In this case, "The whole of what was previously expended in luxuries, by capitalists and landlords, is distributed among the existing labourers, in the form of additional wages."[22] If the population has increased, the additional wages will go to providing their increased demand for necessaries. If not, they will pay for increased luxuries for the working class:

The capital previously employed in the production of luxuries is still able to employ itself in the same manner: the difference being, that the luxuries are shared among the community generally, instead of being confined to a few. The increased accumulation and increased production might, rigorously speaking, continue, until every labourer had every indulgence of wealth, consistent with continuing to work. . . . Thus the limit of wealth is never deficiency of consumers, but of producers and productive power.[23]

Mill believes that the resources diverted from unproductive consumption would be used instead in productive labor, and the consequence would be the distribution of wealth to pay labor more wages. He sees a world that does not need a special class of the rich to provide employment, since laborers would be able to employ each other.

This vision of wealth distributed more widely and more productively, though the source of his greatest error, is also the root of Mill's most famous contribution to the history of economics: his insight that, while the laws of production are limited by the realities of resources and technology, there is no inherent reason that wealth, once produced, cannot be distributed more widely. First Mill describes the constraints within which economies must go about production:

> Whatever mankind produce, must be produced in the modes, and under the conditions, imposed by the constitution of external things. . . . Whether they like it or not, a double quantity of labour will not raise, on the same land, a double quantity of food, unless some improvement takes place in the processes of cultivation. Whether they like it or not, the unproductive expenditure of individuals will pro tanto tend to impoverish the community, and only their productive expenditure will enrich it.[24]

Given the conditions of production, only so much can be produced from a limited earth. Mill fully accepts this aspect of the laws of nature. He knows that productiveness may be increased by science and technology in ways he cannot foresee, but he still holds fast to the reality of limits:

> But howsoever we may succeed in making for ourselves more space within the limits set by the constitution of things, we know that there must be limits. We cannot alter the ultimate properties either of matter or mind, but can only employ those properties more or less successfully, to bring about the events in which we are interested.[25]

Thus Mill fully accepts the ultimate necessity of a "stationary state," achieved when population and economic growth finally hit the absolute limits of the earth's natural resources and capacity to produce food. He does acknowledge that the limits have yet to be reached in his time, but warns (as noted above) that to overlook their ultimate importance is "not only an error, but the most serious one, to be found in the whole field of political economy."[26]

Yet the stationary state need not be a specter of abject misery in which the masses of laborers live on the margins of subsistence. If nations have the will, the fruits of production can be redistributed to benefit everyone. And if laborers will control their birthrate, the redistribution can include substantial amounts of luxury goods:

The Distribution of wealth . . . is a matter of human institution solely. The things once there, mankind, individually or collectively, can do with them as they like. . . . Further, in the social state, in every state except total solitude, any disposal whatever of them can only take place by the consent of society, or rather of those who dispose of its active force.[27]

It is important to note that this is not a matter solely of society deciding to appropriate what an individual has made, but also of society protecting it from appropriation by others, which, Mill points out, will surely happen if society does not prevent it. According to Mill, the choice to allow individuals to keep property is no less a social choice than that to appropriate it from them.

The idea that individual effort depends for its reward on the will of the society is a far cry from the individualism we might have expected after reading Mill's earlier theoretical essay. And it is certainly in tension with the definition of freedom Mill gives in his essay "On Liberty": "The only freedom which deserves the name, is that of pursuing our own good in our own way, so long as we do not attempt to deprive others of theirs, or impede their efforts to obtain it."[28] From the perspective of the contemporary division between the liberal and conservative wings of liberalism, Mill is being inconsistent. Society cannot have both individual freedom and social redistribution, because taking away from some to benefit others is considered a violation of individual rights.

Perhaps Mill does not see any inconsistency because he does not yet really see the implications of pure individualism. In *Principles* Mill seems to balance individual freedom with the utilitarian concern for "the greatest good for the greatest number," though he does not actually use that phrase here. He is not worried about how one decides what is the "greatest good," nor who decides. Like Smith, Mill seems to assume that human persons are inherently social persons, so that social good and individual good are connected, not at odds.

Yet it is precisely Mill's proposal to redistribute the fruits of production that led ultimately to the split in liberalism whereby individual freedom and social equity came to be understood as incompatible goals. The classical liberals, or "conservatives," now understand justice in terms of individual freedom. Any interference with individual freedom, beyond a bare minimum of taxes to ensure defense and laws to secure contracts, is denounced. This view has been well represented in recent years by "Reagan Republicanism" and is articulated in economics particularly by such representatives of the "Chicago School" as Milton Friedman. The "liberals" of liberalism understand justice in terms of social equity and focus very much on distribution. The liberal view is closely identified with the "New Deal" Democrats and their heirs and is represented in economics by the Keynes and his followers.

This seemingly impossible trade-off between individual freedom and social equity has loomed larger and larger as a fundamental problem of social economy, whether in capitalist or socialist-Marxian nations. Accordingly, we will return to it in chapter 6 as a problem that must be recast in order to find what is perhaps a way out of the dilemma.

One final comment on Mill's discussion of the stationary state: Late in *Principles,* while discussing the impact of better distribution on labor, Mill seems to decide that endless growth is not only not possible, it is not even desirable:

> I cannot . . . regard the stationary state of capital and wealth with the unaffected aversion so generally manifested towards it by political economists of the old school. I am inclined to believe that it would be, on the whole, a very considerable improvement on our present condition. I confess I am not charmed with the ideal of life held out by those who think that the normal state of human beings is that of struggling to get on. . . . It may be a necessary stage in the progress of civilization. . . . But the best state for human nature is that in which, while no one is poor, no one desires to be richer, nor has any reason to fear being thrust back by the efforts of others to push themselves forward. . . .
>
> Those who do not accept the present very early stage of human improvement as its ultimate type, may be excused for being comparatively indifferent to the kind of economical progress which excites the congratulations of ordinary politicians; the mere increase of production and accumulation. . . . It is only in the backward countries of the world that increased production is still an important object: in those most advanced, what is economically needed is better distribution, of which one indispensable means is a stricter restraint on population.[29]

Mill continues this rejection of endless growth by commenting on the idea that the world could support more and more people thereby. Mill agrees that this is possible but wonders why we would want to have more and more people in the world. He thinks that room for solitude and wilderness are as important as economic prosperity:

> If the earth must lose that great portion of its pleasantness which it owes to things that the unlimited increase of wealth and population would extirpate from it, for the mere purpose of enabling it to support a larger, but not a better or a happier population, I sincerely hope, for the sake of posterity, that they will be content to be stationary, long before necessity compels them to it.[30]

Finally, Mill sees no reason for "progress" to stop just because the economy ceases to "grow":

> It is scarcely necessary to remark that a stationary condition of capital and population implies no stationary state of human improvement. There would be as much scope as ever for all kinds of mental culture, and moral and social progress; as much

room for improving the Art of Living, and much more likelihood of its being improved, when minds ceased to be engrossed by the art of getting on.[31]

With all his sensitivity to the importance of natural limits and the unique integrity of agricultural land, how does Mill handle the discussion of value? Does his concern for the concrete realities of economics carry over to his further theoretical reflection? The answer is, both no and yes. No because Mill's value theory for the most part follows the labor theory, at least with regard to the cost of production. Yes because, though Mill sees labor costs as by far the greatest cost, they are not quite the only cost:

> The component elements of Cost of Production have been set forth in the First Part of this enquiry. The principal of them, and so much the principal as to be nearly the sole, we found to be Labour. . . . At the first glance indeed this seems to be only a part of this outlay. . . . These tools, materials, and buildings, however, were produced by labour and capital; and their value . . . depends on cost of production, which again is resolvable into labour.[32]

Despite this heavy emphasis on the cost of labor, a few pages later Mill does talk about scarcity as an element of cost of production:

> The case in which scarcity value chiefly operates in adding to cost of production, is the case of natural agents. These, when unappropriated, and to be had for the taking, do not enter into cost of production, save to the extent of the labour which may be necessary to fit them for use. . . . But it is equally certain that they often do bear a scarcity value. Suppose a fall of water, in a place where there are more mills wanted than there is water-power to supply them; the use of the fall of water will have a scarcity value, sufficient either to bring the demand down to the supply, or to pay for the creation of an artificial power, by steam or otherwise, equal in efficiency to the water-power.[33]

Scarcity does, then, add to the cost of production in some cases at least. The above example is a case of natural scarcity in which more labor cannot increase the available water power. Better technology might be able to get more of the available energy out of the falling water, but the amount of that energy is fixed by the volume of water falling at a certain rate. Once that amount is attained as closely as possible, while the demand is still higher, does not the exchange value of the energy then include absolute scarcity value? In this Mill disagrees with Ricardo, insofar as Ricardo consistently assumes that more labor can always be applied with effect. For Mill, as long as there are no available alternatives, the "use of the fall of water" has a scarcity value that is caused by the limits of nature.

Mill asserts, similarly, that rent paid for land on which a factory is built is also legitimately a cost of production based on scarcity value: "And since all factories are built on ground, and most of them in places where ground is peculiarly valuable, the rent paid for it must, on the average, be compensated in the values of all things made in factories."[34] Unfortunately, he agrees with Ricardo that landowners who are receiving rent for more fertile land compared to the worst land in production, are reaping what has nothing to do with the cost of production.[35] I say "unfortunately" because I do not believe that rent paid for the use of the land for factories is any different in principle from rent paid for the use of the land for crops. In both cases, rent is paid because of the relative scarcity of land suitable for the purposes demanded—because of either natural advantages or location near population centers.

Mill seems to be trying to distinguish between scarcity value and value based on relative differences—as when the owners of more-fertile land get more rent than do owners of poor land, because the price for the crops is the same for both. He does not seem to consider that the same happens to landowners who have favorably situated land for factories versus those with less favored land. More important, he does not distinguish carefully between absolute scarcity and relative scarcity. This is not surprising, since it was in his day barely conceivable, even as a matter of theoretical thoroughness, that absolute scarcity would ever become an important problem. While Mill, unlike most, was able to imagine such a day, even he felt it was far off, and could be pushed off even farther by continuous technological innovation and the control of population. In this Mill was right: the necessity of reckoning with absolute scarcity was postponed for over a century. But that reckoning would be easier now if Mill, who did foresee it, had laid the theoretical foundation for it more emphatically.

Finally, it is very interesting to compare an element of subjectivity in Mill's value theory with the absolute subjectivity of the later marginalists. The marginalists, as we shall see, felt they had resolved the problem of exchange value by describing it as entirely a matter of what any given individual is willing to pay for any given commodity. This would be called "subjective utility." Though the concept is very simple from the standpoint of theoretical neatness, its consequence was the loss of any admission of any objective elements into the theory of exchange value.

A generation before the marginalists, Mill was far more balanced in his assessment of value. Though Ricardo ignores the subjective element completely, and insists on the labor theory of value, Mill does admit a subjective dimension, but he does so with some care. According to Mill, exchange value depends on the one hand on "difficulty of attainment" and on the other hand on its "utility . . . in the estimation of the purchaser."[36] To Mill, "difficulty of attainment" includes both necessary labor and the scarcity of the material. This forms the cost of production and must be covered by the exchange value, or it will not be produced. Utility is a matter of both objective use value and subjective desire for the commodity. An exchange value can be only as high as "the utility of a thing in the estimation of the purchaser." This forms the level of effective demand, without which, of course, the commodity will not be sold. From a theoretical standpoint, it is tempting to allow this element of subjective utility to stand alone, since it will cover the element of objective utility: if water becomes scarce, people, who must have water, will place a higher subjective utility on the water. Effectively, it would seem that we can safely ignore the objective element.

Mill, however, does not do this. He does distinguish between subjective and objective utility. While discussing the interaction between supply and demand, Mill comments, "If the article is a necessary of life, which, rather than resign, people are willing to pay for at any price, a deficiency of one-third may raise the price to double, triple, or quadruple."[37] Mill is aware that a high exchange value can arise from the production side, because of the scarcity of "a necessary of life," or from the demand side, because of a high desire for an unnecessary commodity. In both cases subjective utility can be said to be the same, but the cause of the high exchange value is not. Mill uses the examples of a scarcity of water on the one hand and a great desire for a music box on the other. Unfortunately, he does not develop this distinction.

How can we assess Mill's many and complex contributions to the history of economics? As a pure theorist, Mill in the end reinforced the decisions for growth, individualism, and the denigration of the land. Deductive method, sharpened by the concept of *Homo economicus,* helped keep the theoretical focus on the individual pursuit of wealth. Mill's theory of value can potentially lead to the inclusion of land as unique, but it is somewhat confusing and in any case it is buried in the second half of Mill's *Principles* and is not part of his earlier essay on method.

Although Mill himself was very optimistic about the potential benefits of distribution within the limits of the natural world and in the stationary state, later generations on the whole seem to have continued to be pessimistic. Most of the world for the most part has yet to face up to the facts of natural limits. Economic growth is still virtually unquestioned as the only way to overcome poverty. This desire to hold off—or even to escape—the absolute limits of finite life on this planet, fueled by the haunting specter of the stationary state as one of misery for the masses of the world, powerfully reinforces the preoccupation in economic life with endless growth and frenetic innovation. Mill's rosy view of the stationary state clearly has not been seriously considered. Although some headway in population control has been made, largely in industrialized nations, even there it is still heresy to question untrammeled economic growth as the sole goal of economies. (This is not to say that a stationary state should be the goal either, but that the role and purposes of the economy in society should be a matter for discussion.) Mill's proposal about distribution has had more impact; it has been used to provide enough social equity to stave off Marxian revolutions in industrial nations.

It is much harder to assess the contributions of Mill's *Principles,* the standard textbook on political economy for decades in the second half of the nineteenth century. It would be very interesting to discover whether Mill's ideas about nature and agriculture, and about "productive" labor, influenced political economists at all during those decades. Although there is much to learn from Mill's discussion of these issues, and much may have been learned while *Principles* was still widely read, it is certain that the book's potential was never realized in the continuing mainstream development of economic theory. Mill's earlier theoretical work, along with his proposal about distribution, were taken up into the mainstream of economics, but his later, more concrete reflections gradually disappeared from sight, as we will see.

4

For History and Industrialization over Rural Life: Karl Marx

W HILE J OHN S TUART M ILL looked into the future of capitalism and found it good, Karl Marx (1818–1883) looked and found it terrible. Mill thought reform would correct the worst evils of capitalism and could lead to a kind of utopia, while Marx was convinced that nothing less than revolution would end the misery of the working class. Marx appears, then, to be a real radical, establishing a new economic and social theory in stark contrast to classical economics. In some respects Marx *was* radically different, as we shall see.

Nevertheless, with respect to the value choices we have been exploring in the history of economics, Marx is similar to the classical economists in certain key respects. Marx accepts without question the fundamental choice for growth in the production of goods. Though he rejects individualism, he does so in radical reaction to it, and Marxism ends up destroying communities to create "collectives." Marx, claiming to be rooted firmly in the dynamics of actual history, also rejects deductive method, yet he relies on Hegel and Ricardo for his theoretical premises, which govern his interpretation of history. Marx is more difficult to assess with respect to land and nature, and he gives mixed signals about them. Yet in the end his acceptance of massive industrialization as the most efficient means to the greater production of goods, and as the necessary road to communism, means that land and nature will be sacrificed. In that sense, what Marx gives with one hand, he takes away with the other.

All this is not to claim that Marx contributes nothing to the project of critiquing basic assumptions and choices in economics and reformulating them. His interest in history is most valuable; he writes in detail about the connection between the Highland clearances and industrialization, for example.[1] But it is difficult sometimes to distinguish where Marx is simply describing the results of capitalism and where he is agreeing with them. One also wonders often if he is being sarcastic. If he is, the interpretation must be different. Nevertheless, it is impossible to ignore him. Marx offered the only radical alternative to what became the classical-neoclassical synthesis that has been widely pursued by nations. (Such movements as the utopian socialists and the German historical school have had considerable impact in certain capitalist nations like Germany and Sweden, but they have not provided an alternative economic theory that has contended directly with neoclassical theory.)

Marx is important for several reasons. First, and positively, Marx insisted on the importance of history. It is a fundamental thesis of this project that all economics (indeed, all disciplines) need to incorporate a historical-critical perspective. Marx was also right to insist, in contrast to Mill, that production and how people participate in it is at least as important as distribution. Third, Marx did more than anyone else to draw attention to the misery of the masses of laborers and how industrialization was causing that misery. But fourth, and negatively, Marx offers no real alternative to capitalism with respect to the treatment of the land. If anything, his version of the labor theory of value is even worse than what we have seen because it more clearly and more emphatically opposes including land and nature in the discussion. Finally, Marx's theory of dialectical materialism leads him to encourage the destruction of communities for the sake of fostering, not *Homo economicus*, but the opposite extreme (and just as abstract and unrealistic), "socialist man."

Marx reveals his own priorities for political economy in his *Theories of Surplus Value* of 1863. Marx much admires Ricardo's "scientific" position, while accusing Malthus of allowing his allegiance to the landlord class to skew his economics. Marx says that Malthus supported the Corn Laws because "like a true member of the English State Church, he was a professional sycophant of the landed aristocracy, whose rents, sinecures, extravagance, heartlessness, etc., he justified from the economic point of view."[2]

By way of contrast, Marx extolled Ricardo because he was after production, no matter what:

> Ricardo ... wants production for the sake of production, and in this he is right. Those who assert, as Ricardo's sentimental opponents have done, that production as such is not the end, forget that production for the sake of production merely means the development of human productive power, that is, *the development of the wealth of the human race as an end in itself* [author's emphasis].[3]

Marx goes on to deny Sismondi's concern for the rights of individuals, asserting that the only way to develop individuals in the long run is to go through the stage of capitalism, despite the high cost:

> What is not understood is that the development of the capabilities of the species *man*, although it [proceeds] at first at the expense of the majority of human individuals and of certain human classes, will eventually break through this antagonism and

coincide with the development of the individual person, and that therefore the higher development of individuality can only be purchased through a historical process in which individuals are sacrificed.4

Here Hegelian philosophical theory governs Marx's reading of the historical process. Ricardo, says Marx, does not care whether the interests of the landlords or the interests of the workers are sacrificed, so long as production is advanced.5 This is acceptable to Marx because it coincides with the theory that this will in turn advance the whole human species. In this way Ricardo shows his "scientific impartiality" while Malthus "steals" scientific theories only to advance the cause of the rich.6

In these revealing sentences Marx proclaims himself a supporter of the choice for economic growth and indeed affirms quite consciously that growth in production of material goods is worth the sacrifice of individuals. Marx never wavers in this affirmation, and subsequent Marxism has followed it faithfully. In both Marxian socialism and capitalism, then, it is commonplace to assert that the lives of whole generations of persons (not to mention the integrity of whole cultures) must be sacrificed for the sake of economic development. Sociologist Peter Berger has shown that this is so, pointing out how, for the sake of economic development, both socialist China and capitalist Brazil have been willing to "sacrifice at least a generation for the achievement of their respective goals."7

Individual, community, and environmental sacrifice is a choice taken for granted in both theories as a necessary cost of the choice for growth. In both systems it is argued that the benefits of industrialization to future generations will outweigh the pain and misery of the laborers. In both systems the laborers so sacrificed have not been consulted. Even where political voting rights have been granted to all, real participatory power, in the sense of serious debate and choice about the nature of the system, has been absent. In both systems resistance to industrialization has consistently been met by choruses of "You can't fight progress!"

Marx proclaims himself in favor of "scientific impartiality," but his choices for growth and for the working class belie this in the end. In the first place, Ricardo's science, according to Marx, is used in the service of obtaining production. This is not "scientific impartiality" at all, but partiality for production, which is fine with Marx. Second, Marx himself persistently allows his loyalty to the working class to govern his theoretical thinking. Clearly Marx's own political agenda is prior to his theory no less than Malthus's, and in fact more so, because Malthus was almost certainly not conscious of such an influence. On the positive side, self-critical awareness of the role of one's social and economic "location" comes from the legacy of Marx and is growing in influence in many academic fields. Unfortunately neither capitalist nor Marxian economics has engaged in such self-criticism to the degree needed.

Marx is trying to have it both ways. He wants to claim that scientific impartiality points to the ultimate victory of the working class. In fact he has chosen the cause of the working class, and set out to build a theory to advance that cause. From an ethical point of view, this is not necessarily wrong, and it may well be unavoidable. But it is important to be very self-conscious and forthright about one's governing value choices. (There are plenty of biblical and theological arguments for a special concern for poor and vulnerable people, or what is known as the "preferential option for the poor," so many Christians are sympathetic with Marx's choices.) And as we have seen, classical economic theory itself was built around some basic value choices. A postmodern economic theory should be built around a choice for protecting the integrity of human and natural communities in sustainable relation to each other.

But there is a great difference between a critique that includes the proclamation that one's bias is absolutely correct, regardless of any other considerations, and a critique that includes a self-criticism that tries to compensate for one's biases by the inclusion of other voices. Although Marx opened eyes to the built-in biases of any theory, I cannot find evidence in Marx's own writings that he himself had any interest in fostering openness. He wears his prejudices with pride and certainty in their justice, and thereby both misses some implications of his own brilliant reading of British history, and effectively slams the door to possibilities for self-correction. One hopes that Marxists who have come to care about the integrity of the environment will be able to find some toehold in Marx for transformation, but this will be very difficult. The combination of the labor theory of value and the acceptance in Marxism of the fundamental choice for economic growth by means of massive industrialization has led to extensive environmental damage and the systematic destruction of communities throughout Eastern Europe.

Marx borrows the labor theory of value from Ricardo and uses it as the regulator of everything else in his thinking. Despite Marx's insistence on the priority of history, his massive work *Capital* begins with the labor theory of value and is largely devoted to theoretical issues. As we will see, the historical perspective, though full of insight in itself, does not significantly affect Marx's theory.

The labor theory of value is the theory that exchange value depends on "embodied labor" and only on embodied labor. Marx rejects with disdain the attempt of Malthus to talk about the labor theory in terms of the amount of labor a commodity could "command," rather than how much labor was actually embodied in it. As we saw above, the "labor-command" theory allowed some possibility of including a contribution to exchange value from the raw materials embodied in the commodity. But Marx insists that labor and only labor can be the measure of exchange value.

Like the classical economists, Marx distinguishes between use value and exchange value. He defines a commodity as "an object outside us" that "satisfies human wants of some sort or another," and for him, "the nature of such wants, whether, for instance, they spring from the stomach or from fancy, makes no difference."[8] It is important to remember here that Marx is describing a "commodity," which is, according to him, an invention of the social relations of capitalism. Material goods produced for the consumption of the producers themselves have use value, but not exchange value. Marx asserts that the usefulness of a commodity is a property "independent of the amount of labour required to appropriate its useful qualities." However, use values "become a reality only by use or consumption."[9] This way of describing use value defines goods solely in terms of their "usefulness" to the satisfaction of some human desire. This is in no way different from standard classical theory; Marx is no more interested than other economists in any inherent value of the entities of the natural world. They are there to be used, whether in capitalism or under any other economic arrangement.

To Marx, use value is, however, almost irrelevant; exchange value is what matters in capitalism, and exchange value has nothing to do with use value. Exchange value, according to Marx, is a process of abstraction from the material reality of a commodity that is based on a relative and fluctuating relation of a commodity with other commodities. Marx seems to believe that, because exchange values fluctuate, they cannot be based on any natural property of the commodity, since these do not change.

> Hence exchange value appears to be something accidental and purely relative, and consequently an intrinsic value, i.e., an exchange value that is inseparably connected with, inherent in commodities, seems a contradiction in terms.[10]

This means that the "common 'something' [which equates exchange values] cannot be either a geometrical, a chemical, or any other natural property of commodities."[11] Since no actual material property of a commodity determines its exchange value, the only "common something" left is the labor embodied in the commodity.

Marx goes on to claim that "exchange value is the only form in which the value of commodities can manifest itself or be expressed."

> A use-value, or useful article, therefore, has value only because human labour in the abstract has been embodied or materialised in it. How, then, is the magnitude of this value to be measured? Plainly, by the quantity of the value-creating substance, the labour, contained in the article.[12]

If the labor required to produce goods remained constant, their exchange values would remain constant. But they do not. Exchange values change as the productivity of labor changes. Marx, in agreement with classical economics here, says that labor productivity depends on "various circumstances, [including] amongst others, the average amount of skill of the workmen, the state of science, and the degree of its practical application, the social organisation of production, and physical conditions."[13]

What does Marx mean by "physical conditions"? Simply that in unfavorable physical circumstances, the same amount of labor will be able to obtain less of an item than it would in more favorable conditions:

> For example, the same amount of labour in favourable seasons is embodied in 8 bushels of corn, and in unfavourable, only in four. The same labour extracts from rich mines more metal than from poor mines. Diamonds are of very rare occurrence on the earth's surface, and hence their discovery costs, on an average, a great deal of labour time.[14]

Notice that Marx's wording does not leave out a possible role for relative or even absolute scarcity. He does not necessarily assume that more labor will be able to produce the same amount as before. He is choosing to *measure* the exchange value, whatever its source, by labor.

If Marx had made no further claim for labor, his value theory might be adapted to include a role for land and resources. He does seem to appreciate the contribution made by nature to use value:

> Man . . . can work only as Nature does, that is by changing the form of matter. Nay more, in this work of changing the form he is constantly helped by natural forces. We see, then, that labour is not the only source of material wealth, of use-values produced by labour. As William Petty puts it, labour is its father and the earth its mother.[15]

But Marx rules out any relation to exchange value, claiming that a "thing can be a use-value, without having value. This is the case whenever its utility to man is not due to labour. Such are air, virgin soil, natural meadows, etc."[16] Here Marx is following Locke's premise that these things cost only the "toil and trouble" of getting and using them.

So far as Marx is only describing the nature of exchange value in capitalism, his argument contains useful insights. He claims that in capitalism a "commodity" is treated as if it had no material reality: the only thing that matters is its exchange value entirely abstracted from the actual world. Nature is disregarded:

> To what extent some economists are misled by the Fetishism inherent in commodities, or by the objective appearance of the social characteristics of labour, is shown, amongst other ways, by the dull and tedious quarrel over the part played by Nature in

the formation of exchange value. Since exchange value is a definite social manner of expressing the amount of labour bestowed upon an object, Nature has no more to do with it, than it has in fixing the course of exchange.[17]

The social relations of capitalism, claims Marx, measure exchange value by abstract labor, and only by labor. But does Marx mean only to point out the alienating abstractions of capitalism, or does he go on to accept the theory that exchange value and even use value depend on actual embodied labor—whatever the economic system?

I believe that the latter is true for Marx, and I am certain that it is for Marxian economists. For example, respected Marxian economist Ernest Mandel writes that Marxism accepts the labor theory of value as fundamentally true, and not just a description of capitalist social relations. He argues that analysis of the constituent elements of a commodity always finds labor at the bottom of it; logically, natural elements contribute only to use value; and "by reduction to the absurd" we can show that "at the moment human labor disappears from production, value, too, disappears with it [since no one is left to buy]."[18] Even though, again, this observation applies to "commodities," both Marx and Mandel continually slide between what is capitalism and what is normative, and they continually slip into applying the labor theory to use value as well as exchange value.

Although Marx, as seen above, does acknowledge a role for nature in use value, he is much more interested in the role of labor. He describes how labor makes things "useful" and endows things with the properties whereby they satisfy human wants:

> So far as it is a value in use, there is nothing mysterious about it, whether we consider it from the point of view that by its properties it is capable of satisfying human wants, or from the point that those properties are the product of human labour. It is as clear as noon-day, that man, by his industry, changes the forms of the materials furnished by nature, in such a way as to make them useful to him.[19]

This argument could imply that both use value and exchange value are the creation of labor. Use value is indeed partly a creation of labor. And perhaps Marx does not intend to imply that it is *only* the creation of labor. Yet he is not clear, and the tendency is constantly to come back to labor as the focus of attention. (This is not at all surprising, given Marx's commitment to alleviating the mass suffering of laborers. He wants to formulate an argument that will lend support to the labor cause, and he does so by trying to show that capital is congealed labor based on exploitation. Land and nature understandably take a back seat to his concern.)

What is Marx's attitude toward land and nature? Can we get a clearer understanding when he is not theorizing? The 1846 *German Ideology* begins with a premise about human beings very different from that of the other political economists we have considered. While they hold to the myth of individuals existing apart in a state of nature and coming together secondarily for self-interested motives, Marx claims that human beings "begin to distinguish themselves from animals as soon as they begin to *produce* their means of subsistence." This act of production "presupposes the *intercourse* of individuals with one another."[20] Human relationships then are thoroughly rooted in the "materialistic connection of men with one another, which is determined by their needs and their mode of production, and which is as old as men themselves."[21]

In his *Grundrisse* (1857–1858), Marx himself critiques the Enlightenment myth of natural individualism:

> The individual and isolated hunter and fisherman, with whom Smith and Ricardo begin, belongs among the unimaginative conceits of the eighteenth-century Robinsonades. . . .
>
> The more deeply we go back into history, the more does the individual . . . appear as dependent, as belonging to a greater whole. . . . The human being is in the most literal sense a *Zoonpolitichon*, not merely a gregarious animal, but an animal which can individuate itself only in the midst of society.[22]

Marx goes on to describe the development of property from communal tribal systems through feudalism to bourgeois capitalism.

Although Marx clearly understands the essentially social character of traditional societies, he still thinks of them as primitive:

> Those ancient organisms of production are, as compared with bourgeois society, extremely simple and transparent. But they are founded either on the immature development of man individually, who has not yet severed the umbilical cord that unites him with his fellow men in a primitive tribal community, or upon direct relations of subjection. They can arise and exist only when the development of the productive power of labour has not risen beyond a low stage, and when, therefore, the social relations within the sphere of material life, between man and man, and between man and Nature, are correspondingly narrow. This narrowness is reflected in the ancient worship of Nature, and in the other elements of the popular religions. The religious reflex of the real world can, in any case, only then finally vanish, when the practical relations of everyday life offer to man none but perfectly intelligible and reasonable relations with regard to his fellowmen and to nature.[23]

Here again Marx betrays his Hegelian rationalism. He rejects individualism, but his rationalism blinds him to any appreciation of the richness and sophistication of traditional cultures. In this Marx simply reflects the dominant "wisdom" of his era.

Marx seems to think of nature as something inert and unproductive, until human labor makes something "useful" of it:

> Iron rusts and wood rots. Yarn with which we neither weave nor knit, is cotton wasted. Living labour must seize upon these things and rouse them from their death-sleep, change them from possible use-values into real and effective ones. Bathed in the fire of labour, appropriated as part and parcel of labour's organism, and, as it were, made alive for the performance of their functions in the process, they are in truth consumed, . . . as elementary constituents of new use-values, of new products.[24]

Marx rightly insists that the interaction of labor and nature "is the everlasting nature-imposed condition of human existence," and thus will be part of every social arrangement. But he clearly gives the greatest attention to the role of labor, and passes over lightly the role of nature.[25]

The political goal of justifying the primacy of labor and the right of labor to its own product leads Marx to deny the significance of any other contribution. For example, Marx insists that the increased productivity of machinery is due to labor: "Although . . . Modern Industry raises the productiveness of labour to an extraordinary degree, it is by no means equally clear, that this increased productive force is not, on the other hand, purchased by an increased expenditure of labour."[26] Marx goes to a great deal of trouble to develop a theory to explain how embodied labor is really the source of increased productivity. He is arguing with the claim of capitalists that they have provided the means of increased productivity, and therefore deserve a greater share in the profits. In this battle between capital and labor, nature, as usual, loses.

The dependence of modern industrial machinery on high inputs of cheap energy from coal and oil seems to be completely ignored by Marx. The claim that the contribution of coal and oil to productivity gains comes solely from the human labor that went into extracting it from the earth simply does not hold up. In fact, we could say that Marx denies the embodied labor of nature, whereby hundreds of years of the production of living material was transformed into concentrations of carbon energy. Because of his political agenda and the consequent determination to fight the claims of both capitalists and landlords, what Marx concedes to nature he quickly takes away.

Similarly, Marx gives considerable attention to the history of land use and the accompanying condition of peasants and craftspeople in England. Yet what he gives on the one hand in an appreciation of them he takes away on the other by envisioning a better situation on the other side of industrial development. Even more problematic is the unfortunate circumstance that his positive comments about agriculture and rural communities are also generally missed, because they are typically buried in the depths of *Capital* and in the *Grundrisse*, which was not published until much later. Most readers of Marx see first and foremost the statement in the *Manifesto of the Communist Party* of 1848:

> The bourgeoisie has subjected the country to the rule of the towns. It has created enormous cities, has greatly increased the urban population as compared with the rural, and has thus rescued a considerable part of the population from the idiocy of rural life.[27]

In the *Manifesto* this statement is not qualified in any way. The reader is left with the impression that rural life is basically "idiotic," and so, while the bourgeoisie has committed outrageous acts against the working class, urban laborers can presumably at least be grateful to have been rescued from the miseries of life on the farm.

Yet in *Capital* and elsewhere Marx is much more careful. When he refers to rural life elsewhere, he makes it clear that its "idiocy" has been caused by exploitation that has not always existed, and it has been increased by capitalist development. Nevertheless, these qualifications show up in the midst of a defense of industrialization. Marx's interest in massive industrial projects seems to blind him to some implications of his own observations about the history of English agriculture. Marx himself argues that the system of "peasant proprietors," once so prevalent in England, was a very healthy system for both the farmers and the land, while large-scale capitalism is disastrous for both. In the middle of a long discussion in *Capital* on the production of surplus value through the large-scale organization of labor, Marx inserts this footnote:

> Peasant agriculture on a small scale, and the carrying on of independent handicrafts ... also form the economic foundation of the classical communities at their best, after the primitive form of ownership of land in common has disappeared, and before slavery had seized on production in earnest.[28]

Marx goes on to discuss modern industry and agriculture at the end of the chapter. He argues that, although modern industry "annihilates the peasant," it replaces the "irrational, old fashioned methods of agriculture" with "scientific" ones. Capitalist production "completely tears asunder the old bond of union which held together agriculture and manufacture in their infancy," but it also "creates the conditions for a higher synthesis in the future, viz., the union of agriculture and industry on the basis of the more perfect forms they have each acquired during their temporary separation." So far Marx seems to be arguing for the industrialization of agriculture, despite its negative effects on the peasant. Yet in the next sentence he adds:

Capitalist production, by collecting the population in great centres . . . , on the one hand concentrates the historical motive-power of society; on the other hand, it disturbs the circulation of matter between man and the soil, i.e., prevents the return to the soil of its elements consumed by man in the form of food and clothing; it therefore violates the conditions necessary to lasting fertility of the soil. By this action it destroys at the same time the health of the town labourer and the intellectual life of the rural labourer.[29]

Next, Marx goes back again to defending the process of idustrialization of agriculture, because, he believes, it will lead beyond itself to a system that restores the maintenance of the lasting fertility of the soil "as a regulating law of social production," but now at last "under a form appropriate to the full development of the human race." Then (still in the same paragraph!) Marx goes back to his condemnation of capitalist methods:

Moreover, all progress in capitalist agriculture is a progress in the art, not only of robbing the labourer, but of robbing the soil; all progress in increasing the fertility of the soil for a given time, is a progress towards ruining the lasting sources of that fertility.[30]

(Notice that throughout this argument Marx writes of "peasants" and "labourers" as individuals, and does not mention the impact of industrialization on communities as such.)

Marx, then, appears to be fully aware of the consequences of the industrialization of agriculture (indeed, far ahead of most classical economists); nevertheless, he approves of it for the sake of the outcome he expects. What outcome? Marx believes that postcapitalist agriculture will return to preserving both laborer and soil, but will do so on the basis of collective ownership, or "association," as he calls it. In this way agriculture, like industry, will achieve the efficiency of large scale and yet will overcome the alienation and damage that capitalism causes.[31]

Marx is vehemently against private property, and in his *Manuscripts* of 1844 he sets out to describe how the land was gradually alienated from the people. Marx laughs at the Romantics who "shed so many sentimental tears" at how capitalism is breaking up the old feudal estates and treating the land as just another commodity, pointing out that the land had already been alienated from the people when it was taken by the "great lords" of the Middle Ages.[32] Marx's recommended solution—in one of the few places where he offers one—is a return to communal ownership:

Association, applied to the land, has the advantage from an economic point of view of large-scale ownership, while at the same time it realizes the original tendency of the division of land, namely equality. Moreover, association restores the intimate relationships between man and land in a rational way . . . [land] . . . through the freedom of work and enjoyment becomes once more man's real personal property.[33]

Marx seems to be unaware of or uninterested in the common observation that property owned by all is property owned by none and cared for by none. He consistently downplays the role of individual initiative and knowledge in "material life" and concentrates on the increase in productive capacity that he believes capitalism achieves through organizing and harnessing the labor of the masses.

Marx's fascination with large-scale "efficiency" blinds him to the implications of his own analysis. He is well aware that peasant proprietors have a wealth of knowledge and skill that is lost in a large-scale system, and that large-scale methods ruin the land. But he does not question the appropriateness of large-scale "scientific" methods for agriculture. Whereas Mill details the advantages of the attention that the "peasant proprietor" can lavish on a small farm, Marx seems to assume that this loss will be recovered somehow when land is owned collectively.

Although Marx was right about the effects of industrial agriculture on the "lasting fertility of the soil," he was clearly mistaken in thinking that collective ownership would provide the way to restore the relationship of labor with the land, and in thinking that large-scale agriculture is necessarily more productive than smaller, family owned and operated farms. We now know from the experience of collectivization in Eastern Europe and China that "association" tends to decrease motivation to care for the land, not increase it: the collective farms of the Soviet Union, at least, are just as much a factory system that exploits labor and land as large-scale agribusiness in the United States. We also know from long-term study of U.S. farming that Mill was not far off about the superior productiveness of smaller, family owned and operated farms.[34]

Marx was willing to sacrifice communities and land for what he thought would be superior productivity in industry as well as in agriculture. On the one hand, he appreciates the skill and knowledge of the "independent peasant or handicraftsman," and argues that industrialization removes their skill and places it in the machinery, so that people are reduced to interchangeable parts in a workshop which is now intelligent as a whole.[35] On the other hand, he accepts the loss of these "classical communities" for the sake of increases in output.

It is not that Marx is naive or unsympathetic toward communities and persons whose lives are disrupted, or even destroyed, by the factory system. Far from it. He recounts at length the horrors of industrialization, from increased work hours in miserable conditions, to the loss of livelihood for any who refuse factory labor, to child abuse. Yet in the end he supports industrialization and dismisses resistance as a "reactionary" attempt to "roll back the wheels of history."[36] He believes the factory system will create a new breed of stateless workers who are disciplined and ready for revolution.[37] Family and community ties are painfully destroyed, but this opens the way for "a higher form of the family and of the relations between the sexes."[38]

Marx was right that family relations would be damaged and relations between the sexes would be changed, at least to some extent, but he was wrong to think that the factory system would create "stateless" workers. Most working-class people in industrialized nations, whether capitalist or socialist, are as nationalistic as ever. Marx, in common with most moderns, thought that the solution to exclusive and destructive tribal identities and patriarchal cultures would be their dissolution through universalizing. In capitalism the tendency is for individual, family, and community uniquenesses to be dissolved by means of universalizing the atomistic (male) individual, until everyone looks alike, every family is reduced to its "nuclear" unit (with the identities of women and children dissolved into that of the father), and every community is "McDonaldized" in the global economy. In state socialism the tendency is for identity to dissolve into the universalized collective "man," an ideal taken by Marx from Hegel. If capitalism enshrines *Homo economicus,* and places "him" at the center of its economic theory and complex of ideals, Marxism enshrines an ideal of "collective man."

Both images are distortions, both are part of deductive models of how to achieve social "progress," and both are instrumental to the one goal of achieving economic growth. This goal is well stated by Mandel and could as well be a statement of the goal of capitalism as of socialism:

> Only in a society where labor productivity will be developed to its highest point, where an infinite variety of products will be available, will it be possible for man to experience a continuous expansion of his wants, a development of his own unlimited potential, an integrated development of his humanity.[39]

Finally, then, what Marx gives with one hand he takes away with the other. His appreciation of history and concrete context helps him to see clearly how capitalism destroys land, communities, and persons. No one has provided more illuminating analyses of this aspect of capitalism, and no one has contributed more to the fruitful use of historical-critical method in sociological, political, theological, and other disciplines. Yet in the end Marx accepts the cost that he sees so clearly, and accepts industrialization with all its sacrifices, for the sake of economic growth and for the sake of his Hegelian vision of the inexorable "wheels of history," moving to create the new "man."

5

For Scientific Mastery over Living Standards: Marginalists and Alfred Marshall

DESPITE THE POWERFUL challenges made by Karl Marx, mainstream economists in Western Europe and the United States continued to follow the classical tradition until marginalism began to take hold in the 1870s. The marginalists were a group of European economists who worked to clarify economic method. Most prominent in this group were economists Carl Menger (1840–1925), Léon Walras (1834–1910), and W. Stanley Jevons (1835–1882). Jevons and Walras are considered here as representatives of the school.

These economists set out to make economics as much like a science as possible—particularly like Newtonian mechanics—and this meant concentrating on mathematics. Their tool, marginal analysis, remains the most powerful tool of economics and has had considerable influence in Western culture in general. With this tool the logic of individualism found its ultimate expression, and value theory was recast completely within its terms.

The marginalists concentrated almost exclusively on the "demand side" of economics, to the neglect of the "supply side," or the problems of production, that had been the main interest of the classical school. It was Alfred Marshall (1842–1924), at the end of the nineteenth century and the beginning of the twentieth, who put the two sides of economics back together in the "neoclassical synthesis." At the same time, his interests were much broader than those of the marginalists. Marshall's *Principles of Economics* ranges almost as widely as Adam Smith's *The Wealth of Nations* and John Stuart Mill's *Principles*. Like Mill, Marshall has much to offer anyone looking for ways to establish the uniqueness of the land and the importance of healthy communities in economics. But his contributions to economic method, like Mill's, undercut, in the end, his wisdom about economic realities.

A conceptual forerunner of marginal analysis is the *law of diminishing returns*. The law was originally formulated from observation of the application of labor in agriculture: the more labor applied to the same land with the same methods, the less produce each further addition of labor could extract, until the point was reached at which the addition of any more labor could produce no more food. The marginalists observed an analogous situation in the consumption of what is produced, and distinguished the *average* from the *margin*. Jevons puts it in terms of *pleasure*. "The natural law of pleasure is then clearly stated, somewhat as follows: *Increase of the same kind of consumption yields pleasure continuously diminishing up to the point of satiety*."[1] The pleasure given is the *utility* of the item for the consumer. Utility varies, depending on how close to satiety, or full satisfaction, the individual is.

An example Jevons uses is that of water, and here is solved neatly the problem that puzzled Adam Smith: that of necessary water costing nothing and useless diamonds being expensive. Jevons explains how the exchange value, and therefore the price, of water and diamonds depends on the interaction of *scarcity* and individual utility, or desire:

> Water, for instance, may be roughly described as the most useful of all substances. A quart of water per day has the high utility of saving a person from dying in a most distressing manner. Several gallons a day may possess much utility for such purposes as cooking and washing; but after an adequate supply is secured for these uses, any additional quantity is a matter of comparative indifference. . . . Beyond a certain quantity the utility sinks gradually to zero; it may even become negative, that is to say, further supplies of the same substance may become inconvenient and hurtful.
>
> Exactly the same considerations apply more or less clearly to every other article.[2]

Applied to every other article, the law of satiety means that when a buyer reaches a certain point, rather than buy another unit of the same thing, something else is preferred over that next unit. This last unit, the point at which the buyer ceases buying the one thing and chooses something else, is the "margin." It is possible to determine a great deal about the interaction of demand and supply, and the resulting ups and downs of market price, by analyzing the "margin" with the mathematical tools developed by the marginalists and Marshall.

Marginal analysis makes individual choice the center of economic theory. Henceforth, this perspective becomes not only one of several views embedded in economic theory, but the pivot around which everything else turns. Value theory was completely recast in its terms. Gone was the classical interest in the role of labor in exchange value. The marginalists thought that all they needed to know was the value at which individuals were willing to buy (or sell). The focus of attention became the choices of individuals (or firms) in the market.

One important aspect of the individual utility theory of value was that it was originally hedonistic. Jevons in particular founded his value theory on utilitarian hedonism. He cites the work of the German Hermann Heinrich Gossen, who defined economics as "the theory of pleasure and pain, that is, as the theory of the procedure by which the individual and the aggregate of individuals constituting society, may realise the maximum of pleasure with the minimum of painful effort."[3] Jevons is careful at first to define pleasure as whatever any individual cares about in the widest possible sense,[4] but he jumps immediately to a materialistic view: "It is convenient to transfer our attention as soon as possible to the physical objects or actions which are the source to us of pleasures and pains."[5] Notice that we have moved from seeing economics in the work of Adam Smith as a problem of the "wealth of nations," and a corresponding notion of social wealth, to seeing economics as concerned with maximizing individual pleasure in consumer goods.

Jevons directly links his approval of hedonism to his search for a way to make economics a "science" like Newtonian physics:

> In this work I have attempted to treat Economy as a Calculus of Pleasure and Pain. . . . The nature of Wealth and Value is explained by the consideration of indefinitely small amounts of pleasure and pain, just as the Theory of Statics is made to rest upon the equality of indefinitely small amounts of energy.[6]

Pleasure and pain can be measured as "utility" very precisely in terms of exchange value, or market price. Economics can be a science like Newtonian mechanics most easily insofar as it concentrates on market transactions. It would appear that Jevons began with the method he desired—deduction that closely follows Newtonian mechanics—and found plausible premises to fit the method. The circle becomes complete in Walras, who goes beyond Jevons to assert that scientists, having drawn their "type concepts" from experience, "abstract ideal-type concepts" from which they construct their theories. "After that they go back to experience not to confirm but to apply their conclusions. . . . The return to reality should not take place until the science is completed and then only with a view to practical application."[7]

Such a methodology easily leads to attempts to reconstruct reality in accordance with the model, rather than constructing models in accordance with reality. Walras claims that it is legitimate to construct a theory on the basis of experience, but he then advocates applying the theory without checking it from time to time for continued conformity to reality. He seems to feel that, since the "science" is "completed" (perfected), it is safe to apply it without revising it on the basis of how it works out in actual experience.

Walras's view of economic method clarifies how economists have applied rather than tested economic theories, so that the economy is increasingly designed to encourage the very kind of behavior that the theory predicts. Consequently, a self-reinforcing trend has developed in which the "real world" looks and is more and more like the model. To complete the circle, as the economy looks increasingly like the model, economists who do test the theory find more of the behavior they predict, and the model becomes ever more accurate at predicting what will happen in the economy. In such a situation, the only way to break out of the circle is to reexamine the basic premises of the model itself—and this is what Walras says is unnecessary, since the model is based on supposedly timeless scientific principles.

While Jevons and Walras did not articulate the most careful version of individual utility theory, it is precisely those places where they were *not* careful that most reveal the underlying cultural dynamics. Their assertions about the purpose of economics and the hedonistic base of utility theory articulate powerful elements of the culture of capitalism that are still evident a century later. For example, Jevons asserts that we "labour to produce with the sole object of consuming."[8] For Jevons economics has not only become individualistic and hedonistic, it has become consumption-oriented, and all sense of the value of labor—of work as meaningful in itself—has been lost. Labor is defined as "painful exertion of mind or body" undergone solely to achieve goals of consumption. One wonders what an economy might look like that took as a central goal the encouragement of more and more enjoyable work, rather than more and more pleasurable consumer goods.[9] Certainly today's social economy effectively celebrates the pursuit of pleasure by means of acquiring things to have rather than by means of doing work that is interesting.

More careful theorists later purged the hedonism and other obviously value-laden elements from the theory, but they were not able to purge them from the underlying cultural dynamics of capitalism, and individualism and growth remained as controlling values. Jevons unconsciously reveals this continuing role of growth as the unquestioned goal of the economy. Whereas in Smith economic growth was conceived of primarily for the sake of producing to meet human needs, Jevons takes the decision for economic growth almost, but not quite, to its final form:

> As the acquirement of suitable commodities is the whole purpose of industry and trade, the greater the supplies obtained the more perfectly industry fulfills its purpose. To bring about a universal glut would be to accomplish completely the aim of the economist, which is to maximise the products of labour.[10]

That commodities should be "suitable" explains the qualifying "not quite" above. Jevons means commodities suited to "all the requirements of the population."[11] He seems still to assume some objective, subsistence content to "requirements" and that the *whole* population is meant. Only later does "suitable" come to mean simply whatever commodities individuals with money want to pay for.

Considering the purely subjective character that utility theory quickly acquired, it is surprising to discover that one of the originators of the theory, Jevons, does assume an objective dimension to utility. He evidently did not see the implications of his value theory. It seems quite obvious to him that anyone will first and most urgently seek to satisfy the "most pressing wants" of life,[12] or what some call subsistence utility.[13] In fact, Jevons never discusses utility without highlighting the fact that the utility of goods for the poor differs from what it is for the rich. Giving the utility of bread as an example, he suggests dividing the total utility of bread into tenths, and removing one-tenth at a time. The first tenth removed will mean little, but as successive tenths are removed, eventually the one so deprived "will be upon the verge of starvation."[14] As we shall see in the next chapter, twentieth-century economists tend to use trivial, not life-and-death, examples for comparisons of utilities.

However, even though Jevons, Walras, and Marshall all assumed this objective dimension to utility, they apparently did not consider the possibility of including as a priority for economics the problem of how to satisfy subsistence needs for all first, and luxury desires for some second. Jevons believed that the "necessaries" of life were easily obtained, and what really drove economics was the creating of new "wants" that kept production going.[15] Walras acknowledged that a major economic problem was how to get production that was abundant, properly proportioned, and equitably distributed.[16] But, according to Walras, these problems had nothing to do with "science." These were matters of "applied economics" and had to do with social arrangements, which were moral problems, not scientific ones.[17] Marshall seems to disagree with Jevons on this and has quite a bit to say about economics as being concerned with "the material requisites of well-being."[18] However, Marshall is defeated by the limits of his methods. In a discussion of economics, he states that economists deal with "man's conduct under the influence of motives that are measurable by a money price," precisely because it is these that can be scientifically analyzed.[19] Consequently, if the problem "is one on which the general machinery of economic analysis and reasoning cannot get any grip, then let us leave it aside in our purely economic studies."[20] Marshall adds a caution: Economists must remember that these matters must be dealt with by our "ethical instincts and common sense," but he does not say that economists should also search for methods that can bring these less easily measured matters into the theory.

Besides the methodological problems with distinguishing types of utility, there was evidently a political motive for avoiding the distinction as well. Jevons seems to have believed it would have meant defining a low level of subsistence for workers and going along with keeping their wages at a low level:

> I altogether question the existence of any such rate [a natural rate of wages].
> The wages of working men in this kingdom vary . . . ; the minimum in one part of the country is not the minimum in another. It is utterly impossible, too, to define

exactly what are the necessaries of life. . . . It is impossible that we should accept for ever Ricardo's sweeping simplification of the subject, involved in his assumption, that there is a natural ordinary rate of wages for common labour, and that all higher rates are merely exceptional instances.[21]

Perhaps the most crucial consequence of the marginalists' emphasis on their scientific method and its uses has been the excessive preoccupation of neoclassical economics with market prices and with what can be priced. Everything began to be viewed through the lens of marginal analysis, until neoclassical theory would finally define whatever was outside the market, or even outside the immediate transaction between two parties, as "externalities." In a standard economics textbook, externalities are defined as "the costs or benefits of a transaction that are incurred or received by other members of the society but are not taken into account by the parties to the transaction."[22] One externality discussed frequently in recent years is pollution, as when a factory pollutes a river so that the fishing industry downstream is ruined. The production costs of the factory do not take into account the cost of pollution; that cost is external, and so is paid for by those affected by the pollution instead of by those producing it.

Numerous ways of addressing the problem of externalities have been proposed, such as regulation to force factories to install equipment that cleans their effluent more, or fines when they discharge more than an agreed-upon level of pollutants. These methods all result in some "internalizing" of the externalities, which results in more-direct payment of the costs by those who consume the products. Those who argue that it is unfair to make consumers pay more are not taking into account the fact that consumers have to pay the costs of environmental degradation one way or another: either generally, through rising health costs, cleanup costs, and a diminishing resource base, or specifically, through higher and more realistic costs for the specific consumer goods being produced.

Pollution and other forms of environmental degradation were going on long before marginal analysis became a theoretical tool. But the problem here goes beyond the issue of internalizing the externalities. The tool of marginal analysis has fostered a habit of analysis that sharpens and makes central the tendency we have seen from Locke on of regarding the land as "free goods" just lying there for whoever wants to make use of it. Not only is nature taken entirely for granted, it is clearly defined as external to the market, to human activity in general, and to economics as a discipline in particular. When Walras defines "social wealth" as what can bring a price in the market because it is both "useful and scarce," he clearly defines out anything that is useful but also abundant, such as air and water.[23]

As the typical economic argument goes, we do not need to worry about things that are so abundant they draw no price. And when they do become scarcer, the market will signal this fact: they will not only draw a price, but increasingly higher prices. Rising prices will result in more conservation, as happened during the oil crisis of the 1970s. Rising prices will also lead to a search for alternatives such as solar energy and will make such alternatives worth developing. The market is thus a highly efficient utilizer of resources—much better than the public domain, which tends to waste resources. The U.S. Forest Service routinely sells timber-cutting rights for less than market value, and Eastern European nations are proverbial for their wasteful and unhealthy use of coal made artificially cheap by public ownership.

All this is manifestly true. And the method of internalizing externalities is a very useful and important tool in attempts to reduce pollution and the waste of natural resources. But in the long run and in general it leads in the direction of accepting the gradual internalizing of *everything* into the market—of making scarce, "owned," and priced what was once abundant and free to all. Walras, in his discussion of social wealth, notes that the first characteristic of things that are useful and limited in quantity is that they are "appropriable." That is, they are amenable to "seizure and control"[24] and so can be made private property, which can be exchanged for other private property. Anything not thus appropriable is not part of social wealth. Such a definition of social wealth means that whenever and to the extent that formerly free and abundant goods are made scarce and "appropriable," to that extent social wealth is *increased*.

Indeed, this is exactly what the most widely used measure of economic activity, Gross National Product (GNP), does. For example, as water becomes more and more polluted, so that clean drinking water becomes scarce, cities have to pay more and more to find suitable water and make it drinkable, and people start to buy bottled water. GNP registers this situation as a *gain* for the economy as a whole, even though it is a loss for the municipalities and individuals who have to spend money for more expensive water systems. Conversely, if things that are now useful but limited in quantity were to become abundant, social wealth would be *decreased*, according to Walras's definition of social wealth. The fact that GNP measures the *flow* of goods and services in the economy, rather than the *stock* of "wealth," only makes the problem worse. GNP neatly (though unintentionally) follows the logic of Walras's definition of wealth as that which is appropriable and so can be exchanged; accordingly, GNP deals mostly with goods and services actually exchanged for a money price. The more market exchange goes on, the more GNP increases. The widespread assumption is that this measures an increase in economic welfare, or "social wealth," even though it is quite possible that economic welfare could actually be declining.[25]

Walras's concept of social wealth makes the concept of *scarcity* in marginalism a problem instead of a very useful tool. I have argued above that scarcity should be included in value theory—and not just relative scarcity, but a concept of absolute scarcity that comes into play when more labor added cannot produce more because there is no more material basis on which labor can work: when the trees are all gone, more labor cannot find more trees. Utility theory in marginalism allows for this nicely, and in this respect is far superior to the old labor theory of value. But the theoretical problem at issue is not just one of accounting for the role of the growing scarcity of resources in rising prices. It is the way these increasing costs for things that used to cost little or nothing are counted as social pluses in the short term.

An example would be the clear-cutting of forests worldwide, even though sustainable harvesting of an intact forest brings manifold benefits in economic as well as many other terms that in the long run would far outweigh, even measured in market terms, the benefits of clear-cutting.[26] For the few years that the forest is being cut and quick short-term profits are being realized, GNP goes up and many assume all is well. Many nations have engaged in this practice in order to fuel development, only to discover too late that the economic, social, and environmental costs for the long term are terribly high. Large areas have become subject to increasingly destructive droughts, floods, soil erosion, siltation of harbors and reservoirs—the litany of costs goes on and on.[27]

In economics, then, marginal analysis fosters a habit of ignoring both the natural base that makes market activity possible and the consequences of market activity for that same base. It is assumed that air, water, forests, fertile land, and the like can take care of themselves. It is not until they become degraded by excessive or careless use or by pollution, and the prices of the products drawn from them rise, that they become visible. Then the solution proposed is to make them even more expensive, and therefore less accessible to those who do not have the means to pay more than the low prices that are possible when the resource is abundant. The illusion is also fostered that increased market activity means greater economic welfare.

The effects of this kind of thinking are most clearly visible in Third World countries that have been trying to "develop" by increasing their participation in the international market economy, and measuring their "progress" by means of rising GNP. Whenever people leave villages for the cities and join the paid labor force, GNP goes up regardless of whether the people involved are actually better off, even in a strictly material sense. GNP simply does not measure whether the people eat better and are housed and clothed better in subsistence villages, because all these economic activities take place outside the monetary system. Noneconomic measures reveal even more of the blindness of judging well-being by GNP, as they show the social and cultural costs of split families and fragmented cultures. Clearly, better measures are needed, ones that actually attempt to measure economic welfare by means of all economic activity (marketized or not).

The habit of focusing on the "margin" also shows up in many areas of our culture besides economics. Consider, for example, the U.S. medical system. Health care in the United States has for the most part concentrated on dealing with what is called acute care, rather than preventive care. Costs for acute care and for high-tech responses to medical crises such as heart failure have soared. The habit of marginalist thinking means that the deterioration of the arteries through abusive diet, lack of exercise, and stress is invisible until the heart stops. If people took care of themselves all along, much of the expensive crisis care could be avoided. But we are just beginning to think in terms of long-term cultivation of health. Crisis management is still our dominant mode of health care.

The same is true of our communities. The deterioration of social health has also been invisible until community disintegration has become so advanced that dysfunctional families, crime, drugs, and the breakdown of social services have become acute crises. The response has been to deal with crisis after crisis on a piecemeal basis, while continuing the habits that generate them, rather than seeking ways to restore communities to health.

Even those who are involved in social justice movements tend to think in terms of what I call "cultural marginalism," focusing attention narrowly on the "margins"—the places where the problems become visible in the form of distressed people and ecosystems. As society is faced with chronic problems of homelessness, unemployment, school dropouts, toxic waste, rural depopulation and urban overpopulation—in other words, disintegrating families, communities, and ecosystems that seem to be getting worse worldwide—the social welfare and charity systems keep trying to deal with these symptoms separately, but make little progress in finding effective long-term solutions. Tremendous efforts go into alleviating symptoms, but little attention is given to diagnosing and dealing with causes, and even less to finding ways to prevent disintegration in the first place. The underfunding of Head Start programs for at-risk children is a good example: Study after study shows that Head Start effectively prevents major problems later in life, for far less investment than those problems cost society, yet Head Start has never reached more than one-fourth of eligible children because of underfunding.[28]

All of these examples allow us to consider the complex interaction of culture, economy, and theory. There is probably no way of knowing whether "cultural marginalism" provided the context for the development of the economic theory of marginal analysis, or whether it was the other way around, or whether instead a more complex set of interactions with other sources occurred. But it was the economic theory of marginal analysis that enabled me to understand the cultural problem of crisis management in the way described above.

The consequences of marginalism for the treatment of land and resources were touched on in the discussion of "externalities" above, but there is more to be said. Not all the consequences are necessarily negative. For example, Jevons, in a promising comment, makes room for a concept of *disutility*—the cost of removing things like ashes or sewage as a "negative value," and he includes disutility in his mathematics.[29] However, Jevons is working on a micro level, considering only one firm at a time, or the relations between two firms. He does not discuss how to account for disutilities at the macro level, or the level of the whole society. "Disutilities" may be counted as negative for the individual or firm that has to pay for dealing with them, but current methods of accounting assess them as positive for the whole society, as measured in GNP. The reasoning is that what are disutilities to some are utilities, or sources of income, to those who are paid to deal with them. As more pollutants are generated, health costs rise, which adds to GNP. Social and individual welfare both go down, but the economic indicator goes up. If GNP measured economic welfare rather than simply monetary activity, such disutilities of modern industrial life would be subtracted rather than added to GNP.

Walras's attitude toward the land is based directly on his philosophy. He accepts the modern worldview, and so sees the universe as divided between the "blind forces of nature" and human free will.[30] The operation of natural forces, with which science deals, being "blind and ineluctable," are "not amenable to anything but observation, description and explanation."[31] This, presumably, is what economics as a science is about. Since the actions of humans are free, the sum of relations between "persons and things" is "industry," and its theory is called "applied science or art."[32] The sum of relations between "persons and persons" is "institutions," and its theory is "moral science or ethics."

Here is revealed a confusion, caused, I think, by the attempt to make economics purely scientific. Earlier Walras asserted that the "primary concern of the economist is not to provide a plentiful revenue for the people or to supply the State with an adequate income [Adam Smith], but to pursue and master purely scientific truths."[33] Science has to do only with "blind" natural forces. But there is no economics that does not deal with the actions of human beings in relation to "things" and to other persons. When Walras and other economists try to slice off scientific "laws" from human relations, they are trying to describe the relations of persons and the natural world in terms of a scientific method designed only to deal with "things," not living, free beings. By Walras's own definitions, then, he is trying to make what has to be an "applied science," or "art," into a "pure science."

Walras believes that despite the ineluctable character of nature, human beings are able to dominate nature because of their freedom, which he believes no other creatures have. This ability to dominate confers the right to do so: "[A human being] has, therefore, an unlimited faculty for *subordinating* the purpose of things to his own purpose. . . . It is not only a moral power, it is a right.

This is the basis of the right of persons over things."[34] Although Walras is careful to assert that no such right exists between persons, only between persons and things, I know of no widely accepted ethics that holds that power to dominate other creatures *per se* confers the right to do so. Nevertheless, Walras is not alone in this belief, but is simply reflecting the dominant culture of his day.

Human beings have a right to do what they please with nature, he maintains, and in any case there is nothing to worry about: Since land is "natural and imperishable," it "cannot be destroyed by use."[35] While the land itself cannot be increased, its products are subject to "indefinite progress" if "larger and larger quantities of the services of capital goods proper are used."[36] These can be "substituted more and more for land-services though never wholly replacing them."[37] The logical conclusion is that "if a community first takes care to expand its capital, it can then increase its population indefinitely."[38]

This is a good place to take up the contributions of Alfred Marshall, who consolidates the work of the marginalists and incorporates it into the "neoclassical synthesis," and yet, in contrast to Walras, begins with a very different view of the role of land and nature in the economy, and so comes to no such conclusion. Instead of thinking of nature as the inert object of human activity, Marshall claims that "in a sense there are only two agents of production, nature and man. Capital and organization are the result of the work of man aided by nature. . . . Man is himself largely formed by his surroundings, in which nature plays a great part."[39]

Marshall does not take land and resources for granted but includes them as basic to everything else: "The field of employment which any place offers for labour and capital depends, firstly, on its natural resources."[40] Land is more than the place to begin; it is different. Marshall remarks that the phrase, "diminishing return" must be used with caution:

> For when the tendency to a diminishing return from increased labour and capital applied to land is regarded as a special instance of the general tendency to diminishing return from any agent of production, applied in excessive proportion to the other agents, one is apt to take it for granted that the supply of the other factors can be increased. . . . In that respect land differs from most other agents of production even from the individual point of view. This difference may indeed be regarded as of little account in regard to the individual farmer [because of possible alternative uses for individual parcels of land]. But from the social point of view . . . it is vital.[41]

Marshall understands that land regarded from the point of view of individuals (or firms) is apt to be regarded as "simply one form of capital"[42] that has alternative uses just like any other capital. But from a social point of view land is different:

Now if the nation *as a whole* finds its stock of planing machines or ploughs inappropriately large or inappropriately small, it can redistribute its resources . . . *but it cannot do that in regard to land* [Marshall's emphasis]: it can cultivate its land more intensively, but it cannot get any more. And for that reason the older economists rightly insisted that, from the social point of view, land is not on exactly the same footing as those implements of production which man can increase without limit.[43]

In noticing the difference between the social and individual views of land, Marshall, in contrast to Jevons and Walras, is thinking in terms of the common good. He frequently sets the human person within a social framework. Instead of defining economics in terms of the satisfaction of individual desire by the production of goods, Marshall sets a different goal for human activity: "The growth of mankind in numbers, in health and strength, in knowledge, ability, and in richness of character."[44] While this is not the direct focus of economics, Marshall insists that the economy should serve this end and should be judged by its success in doing so. In this regard he worries about such matters as "the growing difficulty of getting fresh air and light, and in some cases fresh water, in densely peopled places."[45] Later he uses stronger language, holding that such deprivations have an economic as well as a social cost:

The want of air and light, of peaceful repose out-of-doors for all ages and of healthy play for children, exhausts the energies of the best blood of England which is constantly flowing towards our large towns. . . . For the sake of a little material wealth we are wasting those energies which are the factors of production of all wealth: we are sacrificing those ends towards which material wealth is only a means.[46]

For Marshall the "health and strength, physical, mental and moral of the human race" are both "the basis of industrial efficiency, on which the production of material wealth depends" and the result of material wealth "when wisely used."[47] These are achieved by gaining the "necessaries of life" in the order of food first, then "clothing, house-room, and firing [fuel]," then rest, and "hopefulness, freedom, and change."[48]

The kind of work done is at least as important to Marshall as adequate wages. The marginalists viewed work strictly as the painful means to the end of consumption, but Marshall looks at the impact of types of labor on the "health and strength" of workers and society. It is this consideration, rather than concern for the land itself, that leads Marshall to assert "a public need in every district for small holdings, as well as large." In a footnote he elaborates: small holdings "increase the number of people who are working in the open air with their heads and their hands . . . they often enable a family to hold together that would otherwise have to separate."[49]

In all of these instances, Marshall reveals a set of values different from those that informed the work of the marginalists. He distinguishes between the "standard of life" and "the rate of earnings." He believes that "the true key-note of economic progress is the development of new activities rather than of new wants" and that "a rise in the standard of life implies an increase of intelligence and energy and self-respect."[50] When the standard of life increases for the "whole population," it also increases "the national dividend, and the share of it which accrues to each grade and to each trade." Because a high standard of life produces healthier and physically and mentally more active workers, it increases "their efficiency and therefore their own real wages."[51] Marshall laments the common practice of measuring economic progress by rising standards of "comfort," "a term that may suggest a mere increase of artificial wants, among which perhaps the grosser wants may predominate."[52] But he does agree that when people "who have hitherto had neither the necessaries nor the decencies of life" gain in "comforts," they will also gain in standard of life. Unfortunately, Marshall leaves the issue at that and does not attempt to develop the implications of his distinction for an economy that has moved beyond the problem of trying to gain basic material needs, or for one that finds it easy to increase comforts for some to the level of luxuries while the standard of life lessens for many.

Despite these broader social and philosophical views, in his theoretical work, Marshall, the master economic toolmaker, designed his tools to fit marginalist specifications, and not to work on the problem of measuring the "standard of life." Perhaps he believed the tools of marginal analysis would eventually make it possible to work on his broader goals. Marshall was optimistic about human nature and progress and assumed that the problems of human and economic development would be solved together. He seems to have been unaware of the consequences of the sharp focus that marginal analysis would bring.

For example, unlike Marx, who understood the threat of capital-intensive agriculture to the long-term fertility of the soil, Marshall assumes that people want to improve their land and will use machinery and chemicals for that purpose.[53] That economic theory itself would be used to encourage the practice of mining land for short-term profit to the point of doing virtually irreversible damage was probably inconceivable to him. In general, Marshall assumes that the improvement of nature and the reaping of profits go hand in hand.[54] In this he thinks of persons as social beings, not just as individuals: as he pointed out, to the individual, land is just another form of capital. But the tool of marginal analysis shifts the focus from social to individual terms. For some decades during Marshall's time economists would be preoccupied with working out the uses of marginal analysis at the micro level, or the level of individuals and individual firms. When in the twentieth century they returned to the question of the macro, or national, level, they would see society itself in individualistic terms, and discuss macroeconomics as a matter of the "aggregation" of the actions of individuals.

Marshall was aware of the dangers of inappropriate abstraction. In a discussion of land tenure in his appendix "The Scope and Method of Economics," Marshall comments that Ricardo has been used inappropriately:

> When attention is paid, not to the principles which are embodied in his method of working, but to particular conclusions which he reaches; when these are converted into dogmas and applied crudely to the conditions of times or places other than his own, then no doubt they are almost unmixed evils. His thoughts are like sharp chisels with which it is specially easy to cut one's fingers, because they have such awkward handles.[55]

At the heart of the search for a scientific method for economics was a drive to find those "principles" and to rid the theory of the historically conditioned "particular conclusions."

Establishing economics on a scientific basis was the first order of business, and to do that required dealing "with facts that can be observed, and quantities which can be measured and recorded," using principles that were independent of conditions and readily amenable to mathematics.[56] Because of this requirement, Marshall accepts the established precedent that "economics" is to be defined as "man's conduct under the influence of motives that are measurable by a money price."[57] Congruent is the definition of wealth as individually held property "directly capable of a money measure."[58]

It is as if the purpose of economic activity and the means of organizing and thinking about economics have nothing to do with each other. Under the pressure of the demand in scientific method for easily quantifiable measures, Marshall does not even begin to tackle the much tougher question of what it would mean to define and measure an improving standard of life, let alone actually to encourage an economy in that direction. If the latter goal had been more important to him than ease and clarity of method, he might still have been able to devise ways to fulfill the requirement of dealing with "facts that can be observed, and quantities which can be measured and recorded."

After all, individual health and community health do have a material basis. Although effective measures, even of simply monetary activity, were decades away, the foundations for what would be included, and how, were already being laid. Marshall did have a different goal for economics than the marginalists, with their celebration of production for the sake of consumption. Yet he did not try to redefine the basic terms of the theory in congruence with that goal. As a consequence, the tools he developed became even sharper chisels than Ricardo's, and severed any connection between his goals and his methods of reaching those goals. The extreme marginalists' orientation toward individualism and consumption, enshrined in neoclassical economic theory by Marshall's honing of the sharp tools of marginal analysis, came to overshadow Marshall's wise views of the broader issues.

6

For the Triumph of the Economic Agenda over Health: John Maynard Keynes and Milton Friedman

A T F I R S T, twentieth-century economics seems much harder to track than the economics of previous centuries. Since economics emerged as an academic discipline in the late nineteenth century, it has subdivided many times into subdisciplines. All these have exploded, with a bewildering variety of activity producing mountains of writing. The arguments of economists over interpretation and policy are endless, the complexities daunting.

Yet most of this activity runs within fairly well defined channels, rushing in the same direction. The goals and methods—first expressed by Adam Smith, refined by David Ricardo, delineated by John Stuart Mill, narrowed by the marginalists, and widened again by Alfred Marshall—achieved unquestioned acceptance in the twentieth century, and both reflect and strengthen dominating characteristics of Western culture.

All the trends we have traced through the nineteenth century reached their ultimate forms in the twentieth. The individualism that the marginalists saw in the narrowest terms, that of choice in the market, was expanded and eventually applied to the whole social economy by means of the "aggregation" of individuals and by the use of the "rational actor" model beyond the sphere of economics. The abstractions of deductive method achieved their broadest expression in the increasing emphasis—in economic policy, economic activity, and cultural imagination—on "money" as the key to everything else. Land and nature virtually disappeared as topics for consideration by economists; when mentioned, they were usually treated as another form of capital, virtually interchangeable with capital.[1]

This intensification of the trend toward abstraction even changed the meaning of economic growth, although the goal itself remained almost universally accepted. In the period of classical economics, growth tended to mean growth in the production of actual material "goods," or commodities bought and sold. In the twentieth century growth came to mean any increase in economic activity, with "economic" understood to mean any activity that draws a money price, whether or not any actual material item is involved.

The mainstream of economic theory, based on the neoclassical synthesis first articulated by Marshall, changed its fundamentals not at all in a century.[2] The Keynesian "revolution" expanded its frame and corrected some of its content but did not reshape it. The basic parameters for economic discourse, so clearly laid out by John Stuart Mill in the nineteenth century, did not change. Indeed, toward the end of the twentieth century, the collapse of Marxist economies served only to reinforce Mill's conclusions.

Mill's assertion that the laws of successful production require a market economy was newly accepted virtually everywhere. Accordingly, the discussion of economic policy focuses on how much redistribution is acceptable or possible without dampening production "too much," however that is defined. Mill's distinction between the laws of production and the laws of distribution has contributed to a split in economic discourse over the laws of distribution. On one side are those who believe, with Mill, that the fruits of production can be redistributed for the sake of achieving greater social equity, and that this must be done through government action. Indeed, following Keynes, these "social equity liberals" argue that economic growth can be derailed by recessions unless the government acts to keep the economy moving. On the other side are those who believe that such intervention and redistribution act as disincentives to individual initiative and dampers to economic growth. These "laissez-faire liberals," well represented by Milton Friedman, argue that economic growth is best achieved when individuals are left to pursue their own interests, free of regulation. Yet they too have acceded to massive government intervention to keep the economy growing. The difference is in the methods and purposes of intervention.

At the root of the controversy are not only economic choices but theological and ethical values. Laissez-faire liberalism tends to attract those who understand justice in terms of individual freedom. Social-equity liberalism tends to attract those who understand justice in terms of social equity for individuals. For over a century these conflicting views have defined the landscape of U.S. sociopolitical understanding, and much economic debate and policy making have been framed within their narrow terms.

Opponents on both sides of the debate, however, are working within the same framework. Both sides accept uncritically the pattern of individualism, abstract-deductive models, and endless economic growth we have seen throughout the development of Western economics. And for both sides this framework has rendered communities and land and nature all but invisible.

SOCIAL-EQUITY LIBERALISM:
JOHN MAYNARD KEYNES AND HIS LEGACY

Over half a century has passed since John Maynard Keynes (1883–1946) produced his most influential work, *The General Theory of Employment, Interest, and Money*, and he still towers over the twentieth century as its most dominant economist. Though he had been working on the issues for years, all his work came together for this book, which was written in response to a single great economic crisis, the Great Depression of the 1930s, and dealt with the single overriding problem of that crisis, massive unemployment. Keynes's great achievement was to refute Say's law—that supply creates its own demand—and to explain how an economy can get stuck at the low levels of production and employment that plagued the Great Depression. His remedy was forged out of the necessities of that situation: Create higher demand through higher government spending to cause the economy to expand again. This prescription for economic growth has been a staple of national economic policies ever since, and in many respects it has been highly successful in achieving its purposes.

Decades after the Great Depression, the consequences of Keynes's solution are numerous. Some are obvious and have been topics of much discussion. One topic, for example, is that no amount of Keynesian spending ever seems to solve persistent unemployment without another problem kicking in—inflation. But other issues have drawn less attention, and these I want to discuss.

Perhaps the most fateful thing Keynes did was a direct result of the crisis of massive unemployment. In casting about for a way to address the problem, he seized on the one tool readily available for manipulating a national economy: money. He felt that the whole problem could be analyzed in fiscal terms—investment rates, interest rates, wages—and could also be addressed in fiscal terms—government spending. In the midst of the crisis, this method seemed to make practical sense. Keynes's theory could be understood; even better, it could be applied readily. It also fit in with the trend of economics that focused on readily available tools and what they could reveal rather than on other important considerations.

According to management expert Peter Drucker, the effect of this was no less than revolutionary: "Keynes redefined economic reality." He did this by using symbols: "Instead of goods, services, and work—realities of the physical world and 'things'—Keynes' economic realities are symbols: money and credit." Most crucial, "Keynes was the first to postulate that money and credit give complete economic control."[3]

Keynes's General Theory is designed to solve one problem (unemployment) by means of one method (fiscal policy) to one end (to foster employment through economic growth). At the outset Keynes claims that his work is more "general" than that of the classical economists, because their work assumes the rare situation of full employment.[4] Then he goes on to claim that employment depends on the relation of consumption and saving to investment. Investment, in turn, depends on the relation between the marginal efficiency of capital and interest rates. Keynes sums up his analysis as "the principle of effective demand." The key is "the community's propensity to consume," which if low will lower the effective demand and so cause unemployment.[5]

The concern of Keynes for social equity surfaces here: he argues that "when our income increases our consumption increases also, but not by so much."[6] Consequently:

> The richer the community, the wider will tend to be the gap between its actual and its potential production; and therefore the more obvious and outrageous the defects of the economic system. For a poor community will be prone to consume by far the greater part of its output, so that a very modest measure of investment will be sufficient to provide full employment; whereas a wealthy community will have to discover much ampler opportunities for investment if the saving propensities of its wealthier members are to be compatible with the employment of its poorer members.[7]

The implication is to urge government spending to foster employment of people at the low end of income distribution. Getting the most for the money is accomplished by providing income to those whose marginal propensity to consume is much higher than it is with the wealthy, which would be more effective in generating full employment.[8]

It does not matter to Keynes what sort of employment is given; the point is to employ people so that they will have an income with which to consume goods and services, not to foster healthy work that builds up the community. In fact, the latter might actually be less effective because it could produce less employment and consumption:

> Ancient Egypt was doubly fortunate, and doubtless owed to this its fabled wealth, in that it possessed two activities, namely, pyramid-building as well as the search for the precious metals, the fruits of which, since they could not serve the needs of man by being consumed, did not stale with abundance. The Middle Ages built cathedrals and sang dirges. Two pyramids, two masses for the dead, are twice as good as one; but not so two railways from London to York.[9]

Later in the book, Keynes reveals his awareness that this is not the best state of affairs for a community:

> To dig holes in the ground, paid for out of savings, will increase, not only employment, but the real national dividend of useful goods and services. It is not reasonable, however, that a sensible community should be content to remain dependent on

such fortuitous and often wasteful mitigations when once we understand the influences upon which effective demand depends.[10]

Unfortunately, Keynes does not find it necessary to explain what a "sensible community" would do to foster less wasteful employment.

In any case, what is produced is unimportant and so is the kind of labor, as long as they serve individual consumption: "All production is for the purpose of ultimately satisfying a consumer."[11] Despite his concern for national employment, Keynes thinks in the same individualistic terms as other neoclassical economists. The purpose of production is individual consumption. The purpose of employment is to provide wages to individual laborers. Investment is a function of the decisions of individuals to save or consume.[12] Even though Keynes is working at a macro level, trying to deal with the economy of whole nations, his methods are framed to deal with individuals (or "firms," which are treated as individuals). As Mark Blaug, a historian of economic thought, puts it:

> In modern macroeconomics we simply posit an aggregate outcome of individual choices in accordance with a definite global rule: Keynes's consumption function, for example, is not built up from individual maximizing behavior.[13]

So, while macroeconomics is not built directly on individual actions, it assumes them, and it does not distinguish any level between that of individual firms and national economies. Consequently, the effects of differing macropolicies on particular communities, as well as on the environment, tend to be invisible.

We have seen that the classical economists were trying to learn how to increase the production of goods, to foster economic growth. Keynes shared their desire to foster growth but saw that the classical economists had been limited by focusing on actual material goods and on improving productivity. The marginalists before Keynes were already beginning to abstract economic theory from any relation to actual material life. With Keynes the method takes on a life of its own, and the abstractions start to become the realities that really count.

Although Keynes concentrated on macroeconomic issues, he accepted all the tools honed by Marshall, his teacher at Cambridge, on microeconomics. Like Marshall and the marginalists, he focused on what could be done with those tools to meet the immediate needs of his day. He was well aware of other important issues, but he did not write a Principles of Economics to attempt to address systematically the whole of economic theory and the relation of the theory to the political economy. Consequently he did not effectively work out the implications of some of the issues he was aware of.

One of the most important issues Keynes understood but did not dwell on was the problem of short-term versus long-term investing and thinking. After commenting on the instability of "mass psychology" and its effects on the market, Keynes notes that "expert professionals" end up doing little better:

> For most of these persons are, in fact, largely concerned, not with making superior long-term forecasts of the probable yield of an investment over its whole life, but with foreseeing changes in the conventional basis of valuation a short time ahead of the general public. They are concerned, not with what an investment is really worth to a man who buys it "for keeps," but with what the market will value it at, under the influence of mass psychology, three months or a year hence.[14]

Keynes goes on to claim that this focus on the short term is an "inevitable result" of the situation: investment markets are organized around "liquidity":

> Of the maxims of orthodox finance none, surely, is more anti-social than the fetish of liquidity, the doctrine that it is a positive virtue on the part of investment institutions to concentrate their resources upon the holding of "liquid" securities. It forgets that there is no such thing as liquidity of investment for the community as a whole.[15]

The whole matter is like a game of musical chairs, or a contest in which competitors have to guess what others will prefer: "We have reached the third degree where we devote our intelligences to anticipating what average opinion expects the average opinion to be."[16]

The few investors who do understand the importance of long-term investments face numerous obstacles and less chance of success than those who chase short-term profits:

> There is no clear evidence from experience that the investment policy which is socially advantageous coincides with that which is most profitable. It needs more intelligence to defeat the forces of time and our ignorance of the future than to beat the gun. Moreover, life is not long enough; human nature desires quick results, there is a peculiar zest in making money quickly, and remoter gains are discounted by the average man at a very high rate. . . . Furthermore, an investor who proposes to ignore near-term market fluctuations needs greater resources for safety.[17]

Keynes elects to regard "the activity of forecasting the psychology of the market" as speculation, and "the activity of forecasting the prospective yield of assets over their whole life" as enterprise. While he understands the pressures that result in speculation, he is well aware of the damage it can cause to a society:

Speculators may do no harm as bubbles on a steady stream of enterprise. But the position is serious when enterprise becomes the bubble on a whirlpool of speculation. When the capital development of a country becomes a by-product of the activities of a casino, the job is likely to be ill-done.[18]

Keynes feels that the United States is prone to this kind of problem more than any other nation: "Even outside the field of finance, Americans are apt to be unduly interested in discovering what average opinion believes average opinion to be; and this national weakness finds its nemesis in the stock market."[19] Despite his clarity about the problem, Keynes builds much of his General Theory around the "liquidity preference" and either accepts it as a fact of life or is willing to put up with it in the face of the short-term crisis of unemployment. One wonders if he considered what would happen if his short-term solutions became the basis for long-term economic policies. I am not aware that he ever tried to pursue policies or write economic theory that would help overcome the problem.

Joseph Schumpeter and other economic historians read Keynes's theory as a "short-run" model created to overcome technical problems. As Schumpeter points out, macrostatics is easier to manage than macrodynamics.[20] Keynes's theory enabled him to hold "technique, resources and costs" constant while he examined income and employment, and this of course made it possible for him to come up with his policy prescriptions for meeting the crisis of the Depression.[21] But the simplification came at considerable cost, according to Schumpeter. First, "it limits applicability of this analysis to a few years at most," and second, "all the phenomena incident to creation and change in this apparatus, that is to say, the phenomena that dominate the capitalist processes, are thus excluded from consideration." Schumpeter agrees with Hicks: "Keynes' economics is for depression." Schumpeter thinks that disciples of Keynes do not look at the careful qualifications but have seized on the simple answers given for the problem of depression.[22] While this analysis is oversimplified, many Keynesians have certainly generalized too much.

Keynes himself admitted that he focused on the tools at hand:

It would be foolish, in forming our expectations, to attach great weight to matters which are very uncertain. It is reasonable, therefore, to be guided to a considerable degree by the facts about which we feel somewhat confident, even though they may be less decisively relevant to the issue than other facts about which our knowledge is vague and scanty.[23]

Granted, economists have to make the best of available data. Yet Keynes seems unaware of the danger of basing policy on facts "less decisively relevant." Nor does he discuss what the more relevant facts might be.

Keynes does seem to have some awareness of the long-term importance of land and resources, a central concern of this volume. But his mention of them is truly minimal. Tucked into his discussion of user costs in relation to capital equipment is this comment:

> In the case of raw materials the necessity of allowing for user cost is obvious;—if a ton of copper is used up to-day it cannot be used to-morrow, and the value which the copper would have for the purposes of to-morrow must clearly be reckoned as a part of the marginal cost.[24]

However, Keynes does not understand land and resources to be qualitatively different from any capital equipment:

> Copper is only an extreme case of what occurs whenever capital equipment is used to produce. The assumption that there is a sharp division between raw materials where we must allow for the disinvestment due to using them and fixed capital where we can safely neglect it does not correspond to the facts;—especially in normal conditions where equipment is falling due for replacement every year and the use of equipment brings nearer the date at which replacement is necessary.[25]

This latter statement is quite true, and perhaps all would turn out well if capital equipment were treated as another form of natural resources. But Keynes does not move in this direction at all. Just the opposite. Keynes treats land and resources as another form of liquid assets:

> It is an advantage of the concepts of user cost and supplementary cost that they are as applicable to working and liquid capital as to fixed capital. The essential difference between raw materials and fixed capital lies not in their liability to user and supplementary costs, but in the fact that the return to liquid capital consists of a single term; whereas in the case of fixed capital, which is durable and used up gradually, the return consists of a series of user costs and profits earned in successive periods.[26]

One might say it is unfair to make much of this, because Keynes was not thinking about land and resources in their own right at all. Yet that is the point: he hardly discusses them. In his theory resources are held "constant," and, as we have seen, the only things that matter are employment and money. He does seem to think that scarcity is simply a matter of economic policy, not an inherent characteristic of natural resources:

> It is much preferable to speak of capital as having a yield over the course of its life in excess of its original cost, than as being productive. For the only reason why an asset offers a prospect of yielding during its life services having an aggregate value greater

than its initial supply price is because it is scarce; and it is kept scarce because of the competition of the rate of interest on money. If capital becomes less scarce, the excess yield will diminish, without its having become less productive—at least in the physical sense.[27]

Keynes, as usual, takes the conditions of the Great Depression as normative and assumes resources are plentiful. The problem was stimulating the economy to use them. The idea that they could ultimately be scarce in an absolute sense and that this is an important economic problem was not at all in view. Keynes shares John Stuart Mill's optimism about human prospects. In his famous essay "Economic Possibilities for Our Grandchildren," Keynes predicts that capital accumulation will do away with economic pressures for all within a hundred years.[28] He does see population as a factor, but does no more than mention it.

In the paragraph immediately following the one above on scarcity and interest rates, Keynes shows his preference for labor over capital and land:

> I sympathise, therefore, with the pre-classical doctrine that everything is produced by labour, aided by what used to be called art and is now called technique, by natural resources which are free or cost a rent according to their scarcity or abundance, and by the results of past labour, embodied in assets, which also command a price according to their scarcity or abundance. It is preferable to regard labour, including, of course, the personal services of the entrepreneur and his assistants, as the sole factor of production, operating in a given environment of technique, natural resources, capital equipment and effective demand. This partly explains why we have been able to take the unit of labour as the sole physical unit which we require in our economic system, apart from units of money and of time.[29]

Keynes's method freezes a given situation in order better to focus on labor and the problems of labor. The consequence is that natural resources and even capital equipment are taken for granted. Mark Blaug understands this to mean that "in the short run relative prices are determined by prime or variable costs and that, over the economy as a whole, prime costs are all wage costs."[30]

These days it is common to read in the business pages of newspapers that the U.S. economy is suffering from decades during which productivity gains and capital equipment were taken for granted, as well as from the short-term focus of the stock market. Businesses tend to focus on wage costs and labor problems, neglecting these other issues. And much has been made of the corrosive effects of "consumerism" on traditional values. The seeds of all these problems can be seen in Keynes's work, whether he intended to promote them or not. Peter Drucker points out that Keynes always said, "We can take productivity for granted, provided that employment and demand remain high." After discussing the reification of money in Keynes's economics, Drucker concludes that "philosophically speaking, Keynes became an extreme nominalist."[31]

Drucker does not specify what this means, but two possibilities are relevant. For the first, I draw on an essay by Charles Blaisdell, who observes that nominalism has tended to claim that "there is, in fact, no world outside of our perceptions, that perception itself is the only reality."[32] In this sense Keynes is a nominalist in his emphasis on the psychology of the market—on such issues as consumer confidence and investor beliefs. A second possibility is that at the foundation of Keynes's economic thinking lies a belief that nothing is inherently connected to anything else, and that consequently economics can be treated as a matter of manipulating large aggregates. Both of these beliefs combined obscure the fact that economies depend on mediating organizations that connect natural and social systems and that involve complex relationships.

LAISSEZ-FAIRE LIBERALISM: FRIEDMAN AND TWENTIETH-CENTURY INDIVIDUALISM

If Keynes exemplifies an extreme of nominalism, Milton Friedman (born 1912) differs only in emphasizing the voluntarist side, of which laissez-faire liberalism is the prime socioeconomic form. Friedman's philosophical grounding and value choices are easier to find than Keynes's. Keynes was focused on the practical problem of unemployment in the Great Depression, but Friedman begins with his philosophical choices and builds his economics self-consciously on them.

Above all, Friedman accepts classical liberalism, which "emphasized freedom as the ultimate goal and the individual as the ultimate entity in the society." He accepts government intervention, but not for the sake of equity: "We do not wish to conserve the state interventions that have interfered so greatly with our freedom, though, of course, we do wish to conserve those that have promoted it."[33] Individual liberty is the self-professed central value choice of Friedman and the other economists who follow the laissez-faire stream of liberalism:

As liberals, we take freedom of the individual, or perhaps the family, as our ultimate goal in judging social arrangements. . . . There are . . . two sets of values that a liberal will emphasize—the values that are relevant to relations among people, which is the context in which he assigns first priority to freedom; and the values that are relevant to the individual in the exercise of his freedom, which is the realm of individual ethics and philosophy.[34]

At stake here is the definition of freedom, which in turn defines the economic issues. Friedman defines freedom in purely individualistic terms and emphasizes the aspect of freedom that attends to individual liberty from direct control by others. (In this way, not only is Friedman's understanding of the human person narrowly individualistic, but it considers only part of individual freedom and ignores the aspect of freedom that involves freedom to contribute individual gifts and abilities to others. This is one underlying reason for the seeming lack of interest in unemployment in laissez-faire views. When we define freedom as freedom from coercion, we do not see clearly that unemployment is a denial of freedom for contribution, for meaningful participation in society, and so do not realize that unemployment is a denial of individual liberty just as much as coercive regulations are.) For Friedman, this narrow form of individual liberty—freedom from—is the controlling good, and hence political coercion of the individual is the ultimate evil.

Seen in these terms, there can be only two kinds of economy: "One is central direction involving the use of coercion . . . The other is voluntary co-operation of individuals—the techniques of the market place."[35] The latter form of economy depends on the "proposition that both parties to an economic transaction benefit from it, *provided the transaction is bi-laterally voluntary and informed*" [emphasis in original].[36] Friedman would agree that this latter proviso is the ethical foundation of his socioeconomic theory: freedom of individual choice is guaranteed only if the choice is "voluntary" and "informed." This view is commonplace among neoclassical economists and is often cited in defense of competitive capitalism.

But for the most part it functions as an assumption, not as a criterion by which to judge an economic system. The assumption that economic choices are always voluntary is based on a reality that may once have existed but must now be called into question. According to Friedman,

> Each household uses the resources it controls to produce goods and services that it exchanges for goods and services, on terms mutually acceptable. . . . Since the household always has the alternative of producing directly for itself, it need not enter into any exchange. . . . Co-operation is thereby achieved without coercion.[37]

If this were actually the case, it would be difficult to fault Friedman's economic theory on his own terms. But how many households actually do have access to adequate natural resources to produce directly for themselves? How many communities do? Without the means of subsistence as a viable alternative, people must sell their labor in the market to live; they do not have an alternative.

As discussed in chapter 2, in Adam Smith's day there were still "common lands," which anyone could use for subsistence. They were still extensive enough to pose a problem to the owners of the new industries, who complained that people preferred living off the land to laboring in the factories. As more and more of the commons were enclosed, it became harder and harder for people to produce directly for themselves.[38]

I believe that this myth of self-sufficiency remains powerfully operative in the imaginations of economists and in the culture, as its presence in Friedman's work illustrates. It is rooted in nominalism and Newtonian physics, applied to human persons now defined as self-existent individuals. When discussing the assumption, Friedman does not refer to history at all to bolster his argument; he goes directly to the myth of Robinson Crusoe:

> In its simplest form, such a society consists of a number of independent households—a collection of Robinson Crusoes, as it were. Each household uses the resources it controls to produce goods and services that it exchanges . . . on terms mutually acceptable to the two parties to the bargain.39

(Friedman's substitution of "household" for "individual" might seem less individualistic than it is. Friedman's use of the te rm makes it clear that Robinson Crusoe is sole head of the "household," and everyone else [the man called "Friday"] is dependent on him and subsumed under his individuality. This patriarchal thinking makes it possible to treat each household, and ultimately each firm or corporation, as an individual represented by the male head.)

Friedman does not discuss the fact that for many, subsistence outside the market is no longer an option. But he slides into it in his next move, when he qualifies his assertion that people always have this option. The proviso was originally defined as requiring that market transactions be voluntary, and the example of Robinson Crusoe showed that refraining from any market participation was meant. But on the very next page, Friedman jumps from a "simple" economy to "the complex enterprise and money-exchange economy." Here he says that

> co-operation is strictly individual and voluntary provided: (a) that enterprises are private, so that the ultimate contracting parties are individuals and (b) that individuals are effectively free to enter or not to enter into any particular exchange, so that every transaction is strictly voluntary.40

Suddenly the proviso no longer means freedom to enter or not to enter the market for livelihood; it means the freedom to enter or not to enter into any single exchange, and the reality that people may have been coerced into entering into exchanges in general has been tacitly accepted without comment. This means that Friedman de facto accepts that people may be coerced to sell their labor in the market because they no longer have the alternative of subsistence. Despite his claim to put individual liberty ahead of all other values, Friedman in fact limits individual liberty by accepting the dominance of the market system, which is thereby revealed to be his controlling value. Instead of discussing this issue, he passes it off by claiming that the "employee is protected from coercion by the employer because of other employers for whom he can work."[41] The definition of mutual benefit—the ethical foundation of this economic theory—has been changed radically.

If the exchange really is "bi-laterally voluntary and informed," and is part of a system in which the decision not to make exchanges is possible, I agree with Friedman that it "gives people what they want instead of what a particular group thinks they ought to want."[42] Unfortunately, this proviso is being used as a legitimating assumption, not a criterion with which to judge the system.

Friedman also asserts that the market "permits wide diversity," in contrast to governments, which tend toward enforced conformity.[43] True indeed, if we limit our contrast to governments. But when capitalist economies are compared to more community-based market economies and the differences between them in goods and cultural richness, we can see that contemporary capitalist economies, far from producing diversity, are in crucial respects severely limiting it. The capitalist economy does promote diversity, just as it promotes individual freedom, but it does both within a very narrow range. The rich diversities, both in goods and in culture, that once existed, have been narrowed. The results can be seen in such phenomena as cookie-cutter, look-alike housing in suburbia; the increasing similarity of communities, with identical chain stores for restaurants, hardware stores, bookstores, malls, and so on; the loss of regional and local distinctiveness across the world as advertising-driven American culture takes over; the loss of distinctive, locally made products. Perhaps most troubling of all is the loss of genetic diversity that capital-intensive industrial farming promotes, with its heavy emphasis on monocropping for a few varieties of food. Many varieties of corn, tomatoes, potatoes, and many other food crops are disappearing, leaving U.S. agriculture (and increasingly, world agriculture) vulnerable to new diseases and less able to respond to new climate and soil conditions.[44]

Throughout his discussion Friedman limits his imagination by considering solely the results of command economies run by governments. Because of this, he has confused an "independent economy," largely free of government regulation, with "economic independence," which is quite another matter. To see the distinction, we can look to the tradition in the nineteenth-century United States of a market economy based on the community and family farms, rooted in Jeffersonian ideals. Jefferson believed that democracy and freedom are best safeguarded by farmers who own their own land, in contrast to the "mobs of great cities" who are economically dependent and therefore susceptible to "subservience and venality."[45] Widespread ownership of property fosters a society of citizens who

> may safely and advantageously reserve to themselves a wholesome control over their
> public affairs, and a degree of freedom, which, in the hands of the canaille of the

cities of Europe, would be instantly perverted to the demolition and destruction of everything public and private.[46]

Jefferson's convictions were influential for well over a hundred years, as can be seen by the way the western portions of the continent were settled, through the Homestead Acts, in family farms designed to create largely self-supporting communities—in great contrast to the export-oriented plantations of the southern tier of states.[47] My intent here is not to look back with nostalgia to a bygone pastoral era, but to note that there has existed a healthy alternative to the type of all-embracing capitalist system that Friedman supports. This alternative and its applications require much more study, but I want to point out that this community-based market economy did meet Friedman's own proviso about voluntary exchange, and it also, in contrast to Friedman's model, provided for local control of productive resources, which is the main issue, not family farms per se (which if solely export-driven become just as economically dependent). Friedman ignores this issue, despite the fact that it is basic to the question of human freedom.

Although Friedman accepts coercion on the production side, he is not insensitive to the criticism that people without dollars to spend in the market are not free to participate in it from the consumption side. He proposes as a practical remedy a negative income tax, which would give "help in the form most useful to the individual, cash."[48] He likes this remedy because, unlike corporate taxes, farm subsidies, and the like, it does not distort market forces. He is thinking of freedom as expressed by individual consumption of market goods, not as exercised from a base of ownership and control of resources. Giving people enough "cash" to live on, whether via a negative income tax, or by other forms of transfer payments (as favored by Keynesians), might grant people a basic dignity. But allowing people to choose what goods to buy, with no hope of meaningful employment or other way of participating in the creative making of life in their communities, is a narrow sort of freedom. It is, however, consistent with the emphasis in the whole liberal tradition, beginning with John Stuart Mill, of trying to solve the equity problem through distribution, while leaving questions of production and participation untouched.

If Friedman's controlling philosophy of nominalism/voluntarism leads to such a constricted idea of freedom, what happens to land and nature? Friedman hardly mentions them. He does bring up pollution as a case where "strictly voluntary exchange" is impossible:

This is the problem of "neighborhood effects." . . . The man who pollutes a stream is in effect forcing others to exchange good water for bad. These others might be willing to make the exchange at a price. But it is not feasible for them, acting individually, to avoid the exchange or to enforce appropriate compensation.[49]

Presumably, it is in such a case appropriate for government to step in, but Friedman is very reluctant to allow it. Still, unlike many economists who argue for "internalizing" these "externalities" into the market, he does at least mention the possibility of neighborhood action "to avoid the exchange," or the initial pollution, as an option the neighbors might prefer to compensation for damage.

Friedman is quite consistent about his value choices and their priority. One comes away feeling certain that for him, if individuals choose to pollute "their" land and destroy the long-term fertility of "their" soil, that is quite all right, until and unless their actions affect the property of other individuals. If enough individuals care about preserving their land, they will. If not, members of the next generation will have to cope as best they can. His argument that individuals will take better care of their property than government has some merit, except that we can see in agriculture how economic pressures are forcing farmers to exploit their land as badly as agribusiness. Those who are economically dependent on outside forces cannot resist those pressures. An independent economy does not guarantee individual and community freedom; only economic independence can do that.

It is hardly surprising that Friedman pays scant attention to land and nature, as his methodology stands squarely in the deductive tradition and reaches a new level of radical abstraction. In his influential essay, "The Methodology of Positive Economics" (1953), Friedman follows nominalism/voluntarism to its logical conclusion and asserts that the truth of assumptions is irrelevant to the real issue: accurate predictions.

> Truly important and significant hypotheses will be found to have "assumptions" that are wildly inaccurate descriptive representations of reality, and, in general, the more significant the theory, the more unrealistic the assumptions (in this sense). The reason is simple. A hypothesis is important if it "explains" much by little, that is, if it abstracts the common and crucial elements from the mass of complex and detailed circumstances surrounding the phenomena to be explained and permits valid predictions on the basis of them alone. To be important, therefore, a hypothesis must be descriptively false in its assumptions; it takes account of, and accounts for, none of the many other attendant circumstances, since its very success shows them to be irrelevant for the phenomena to be explained.[50]

This argument is completely in keeping with the development of quantum mechanics in physics, which succeeds by dropping the question of "reality" and "truth" entirely and going after statistically accurate predictions. It is a thoroughly congenial method for pragmatic Americans: If it works, who cares how it works?

Unfortunately, none of the arguments I have seen has taken seriously the question of when "other attendant circumstances" are important enough to warrant changing the assumptions. The examples given to dismiss this issue are often trivial, and Friedman's are no different:

> Why is it more "unrealistic" in analyzing business behavior to neglect the magnitude of businessmen's costs than the color of their eyes? The obvious answer is because the first makes more difference to business behavior than the second. . . . Clearly it can only be known by comparing the effect on the discrepancy between actual and predicted behavior of taking the one factor or the other into account.[51]

Friedman is correct that any hypothesis must leave out much in order to be useful. But his argument against examining basic assumptions is not strengthened by his use of a trivial example. Friedman is arguing that no matter what the assumptions are, in the end it is the accuracy of prediction that counts. (If this is so, why not allow those who care about the realism of assumptions to have their way? If assumptions are unimportant, what harm could there be in having more realistic ones?)

But suppose that the "how it works" is not a consequence of the neglected "other circumstances" being irrelevant, and that the method predicts successfully because the circumstances are changed to fit the method—to make the model work. Isn't it rather circular to predict that businesspeople will act so as to maximize their profits, and then reward those who do so, in order that the reality will increasingly match the model? Might it not be the case that, far from showing that people always naturally act in their self-interest, and that this leads them naturally to maximize profits, the theory instead shows that people will respond according to how they are rewarded, whether or not it is in their own best interest? Prior to capitalist economies, people were not systematically rewarded for maximizing profits, and they did not. The model assumes that when people are left free to do what they wish, they will act to maximize profits, but are they being "left free" any more than they were before, or are they just being rewarded for different behavior?

Now taking the model on its own terms, neoclassical theory assumes that the how of profit maximization is through individual-utility maximization (the "rational actor," or *Homo economicus*), but this assumption is not tested. Friedman argues that it need not be, but suppose it turned out that in fact profits are best maximized by a mix of incentives for cooperative and self-denying behavior as well as for competitive and self-rewarding behavior, and further, that when too many businesspeople act only in their perceived individual self-interest, profits are lost? Would it not be important to change the basic assumption to include a more accurate definition of human behavior? These are surely not irrelevant questions.

The issue of basic assumptions is also taken up by Lionel Robbins in his essay "The Nature and Significance of Economic Science" (1935) and is also treated in a trivial fashion:

> Psychology, it is said, advances very rapidly. If, therefore, Economics rests upon particular psychological doctrines, there is no task more ready to hand than every five years or so to write sharp polemics showing that, since psychology has changed its fashion, Economics needs "rewriting from the foundations upwards."[52]

Robbins goes on to complain that critics especially like to pick on the hedonism of the utility theory of value, when only the early formulators of the theory used hedonism.[53]

It is true that the rational-actor assumption does not require hedonism—individuals might consider benevolence to be in their self-interest as much as selfishness. But I have seen many cases in which economists as well as others in the culture still assume that hedonism is what is really meant, or that put selflessness to one side of economic behavior, and reserve it for nonbusiness arenas such as charity.[54] More crucial, neoclassical theory still enshrines selfishness (not simply self-interest) in the theory through the doctrine of asatiety, or the assertion that human desires are insatiable.[55]

Furthermore, even without hedonism, the rational-actor assumption is still radically individualistic, rooted in the extreme nominalism/voluntarism of the Enlightenment. This individualism has gone so far that it has become impossible to discuss social issues in terms of the theory, as Kenneth Arrow has so ably shown. He argues that individual choices cannot be aggregated to find a social choice, nor can individual choices be compared:

> From a formal point of view, one cannot distinguish between an individual's dislike of having his grounds ruined by factory smoke and his extreme distaste for the existence of heathens in Central Africa. It is the ordering according to values which takes into account all the desires of the individual, including the highly important socializing desires, and which is primarily relevant for the achievement of a social maximum. The market mechanism, however, takes into account only the ordering according to tastes.[56]

Arrow has shown that when individualism is enshrined in the foundation of the theory and governs the economy, it becomes impossible to discuss objective criteria for economic welfare. Some economists go so far as to insist that there can be no such thing, as if the economic requirements for even basic survival (as in per capita calories, for example) were unknowable. But neither the theory nor the actual market system based on it takes into account the difference between an economy in which many people are starving while a few are rich, and one in which everyone has enough to live on. For example, it is possible for two nations to have the very same GNP, yet each have one of the two economic situations just described. Another measure, Pareto optimality, also does not distinguish these two conditions—either one could be at a Pareto optimum position. (Pareto optimality says that an economy is efficient when at least some can become better off without anyone becoming worse off.) Keynes showed how the market does not take this into account: the market goes on working with the laws of supply and demand whether the level of market activity is high with high employment or low with low employment.

In the two hundred years since the Enlightenment, not only psychology but also sociology, anthropology, biology, and now even physics have moved away from the atomism of that period. It is now understood that not even atoms are unrelated and self-existent, let alone human persons. Economics needs to learn from these social and natural sciences and reexamine the foundational assumptions of two hundred years ago in a way that is reflected in the basic formulations of economic theory and economics textbooks.

Conclusion: The Choices for Health over Wealth of Nations

THE ECONOMICS that emerged triumphant at the end of the twentieth century, based on neoclassical economic theory, developed out of a long historical process of refinement. The quest for clarity of method and some measure of control of economies was achieved. The greatest goal—learning how to evoke and harness human desire to achieve the production of the maximum possible amount of commodities—was attained with spectacular success.

This success of capitalism in doing exactly what economic theory says it is supposed to do can be taken as empirical evidence that human societies can achieve agreed-upon goals. When Adam Smith set out to inquire into how to help nations generate more wealth, he could not have dreamed how successful the endeavor would be.

No other economic system in all of human history has been so efficient at generating commodities for consumption. Over the course of two hundred years economics has narrowed its purpose to this one, all-important aim. As Keynes put it, the one goal of all production is consumption. The consequences of this single-mindedness are manifold. Capitalist economies, like the broom of the fabled sorcerer's apprentice, march to give their societies exactly what they ask for: ever mounting arrays of goods that are ever more sophisticated and exciting. But the time for examining the goals of capitalism and facing up to the very urgent problems is long overdue. The sorcerer's apprentice thought to avoid the chore of bringing in buckets of water by commanding the broom to do it for him—only to be inundated by the overzealous broom's refusal to stop. In capitalist economies the damage to human and natural communities also grows swiftly. We have enshrined one goal for economies—growth in production—and we have achieved great success. But at the same time, all over the world human communities and natural ecosystems are unraveling under the impact of industrialization, and the benefits are persistently uneven.

Can we harness the capitalist dynamo and direct all that energy in healthier ways? The Marxian attempt to reject capitalism has apparently failed. Revolutions may reverse oppressions, but they seem usually to continue them in the same mold. In Western nations, reforms have helped greatly to ease the pain of industrialization, but the damage continues to mount. Since rejection and revolution have proven ineffective, and reform is not enough, we should accept the reality of capitalist success and ask ourselves how to *transform* it. There are some clues in the failure of Marxism, and in the economic history we have been reviewing, that can help us to reconceptualize and transform free-market capitalism. Forces are already at work that are beginning the kinds of transformation that are needed. The task will be daunting, but we can take heart from the fact that capitalism itself was part of a movement to broaden participation in Western economies and wrest control from the elite few who controlled economic life under mercantilism.

A great deal can be accomplished by changing the use of existing methods, such as accounting practices. But these practices will not be changed unless a change in basic values takes place. GNP should be transformed into Daly and Cobb's proposed Index of Sustainable Economic Welfare (ISEW), a measure that does everything GNP (or GDP) does, but counts negative effects on communities and ecosystems as minuses instead of pluses.[1] This will not happen until there is widespread agreement that GNP is not useful—and indeed is harmfully used when increasing GNP is held up as a primary economic goal even when it has nothing to do with improving actual economic welfare. We won't know how much capitalist economics needs to change—or how much it can be changed—until we actually begin to work from different value choices, assumptions, and goals. Transformation in principle means working from where you are and starting with the methods and tools you have at hand. But gradually, as current economic practices, tools, and theories are shown to be inadequate to specific goals, different methods will be devised, and the whole body of economics will be transformed from the inside out.

In this concluding chapter I offer some proposals to help lay some conceptual foundations for transforming Western culture, capitalist economies, and economic theory. First I look to the economists we have reviewed, to give my assessment of both their contributions and the ways they missed opportunities that we may want to recover. This assessment will provide the basis for proposing some different foundational assumptions and value choices that could help shape the transformation of both the social economy and the discipline of economics. I am not able to spell out all the implications of these proposals, and certainly cannot work out all the problems. That work remains for any who wish to follow up on testing, developing, refining, and correcting these proposals—or making other, better, proposals. For example, the problem of how far the goal of "health" could be quantified for the sake of making it a foundation of economic statistics is very complex and would have to be debated and experimented with. I only propose that it shows promise of usefulness, since health, unlike "the common good," does have quantifiable dimensions even when it cannot be reduced to them, and health as a goal could have powerful positive effects in the wider culture as well. I do hope that others will take up the questions I am raising and take them further than I can. Finally, in the last section I describe some of the theological and philosophical foundations that underlie the cultural, socioeconomic, and economic theory aspects of our situation.

LEARNING FROM THE HISTORICALLY IMPORTANT ECONOMISTS

What can we learn from these economists who have so profoundly shaped capitalism? What do we need to recapture from their work that has not been adequately developed, and what do we need to recast in terms better suited to the new circumstances that will shape the world for generations to come?

Adam Smith set out to inquire into the "nature and causes of the wealth of nations," so that societies could become more intentional about organizing themselves to generate more wealth. He argued against the mercantilist notion that wealth depends on "money" (in the form of gold and silver) and worked to free economic policies so that real wealth, as he saw it—real goods with actual use value—could be produced. He would never have dreamed that two hundred years later wealth would come to be defined in terms of an even more abstract form of "money," and so economic thinking would, in a sense, have come full circle.

Another important element of Smith's thinking is the concept of *participation*. Smith's work can be seen as part of the broad historical movement that has worked for some centuries now to broaden participation in political, economic, and social structures for more and more groups. The rise of capitalism was part of the movement to broaden participation to include the bourgeoisie. Smith described it in terms of the functioning of a local market. In contrast to the distant control exercised in mercantilism—which was clumsy, inefficient, and often not in the best interest of the local people—a community-based free market allows local people to make their own decisions about the matters that directly affect them. Because they know those matters intimately, they can act in their own interest far more efficiently than distant authorities can. In this Smith was right, as the massive failure of Marxism in Eastern Europe bears out, as well as the successful improvement of the economy in China by means of loosening central controls on local markets.

Smith also made a contribution to method that might have been developed differently but was not: He picked up on the Physiocrats' interest in the circulation of the blood as a metaphor for thinking about the circulation within the economy of goods and services. The idea of looking to living natural systems to learn about how a healthy system functions was very good—but biology was in its infancy, and ecology had not been developed at all. In the long run, instead of looking to living systems for models, economists looked to physics, and Newtonian physics provided a mechanistic model. With the mechanistic model came the view of nature as inert and passive—just lying there, as it were, waiting to be made "useful" by human labor.

This supposed passivity of nature played into the attitude toward labor that Smith picked up from Locke and that eventually came to dominate neoclassical economics: that labor is simply the "trouble" of getting resources and making them useful. This led to the paradox that human beings were considered the only actors in relation to passive nature, yet labor was despised and every effort made to escape it. That labor should be conceived as necessary "trouble," rather than as an intrinsically rewarding though difficult activity, is one of the great tragedies of industrialization. Smith was well aware of the danger of the division and specialization of labor, remarking that, taken too far, division and specialization make work deadly boring and dull the minds of those forced to do it. But he never did anything about it. Evidently, the goal of creating more goods more cheaply was valued far more highly than the goal of finding ways to keep labor interesting and challenging. Perhaps that would not have been possible at the time, but now business is finding that interested labor is much more productive labor, and many ways to increase the participation of workers in decisions about how they do their work are being devised.

Smith chose the goal of growth in the production of goods, and he worked to broaden participation in the economy through a freer market system. He accepted the developing factory form of industrialization and ignored the consequent destruction of traditional communities. He chose the labor theory of value over a land-based theory, thus paving the way for the later disappearance of land as a unique factor in its own right. Finally, his description of the interaction of the decisions of individuals in a local market, while assuming a social context, later became the basis of the development of the atomistic individualism that still dominates neoclassical economic theory.

The Wealth of Nations left doors open for economics to develop in various ways. But Ricardo inadvertently closed most of those doors when he chose deductive method, which consequently became the tool for developing economics. John Stuart Mill firmly set the direction of this development when he enshrined *Homo economicus* as the center of the theory. Deductive method is useful, important, and unavoidable, but it needs to be used appropriately. To abstract the method from any ongoing relationship with historical context and empirical research—to allow deductive theory to drive the system instead of placing it firmly in both time and place and allowing experience and changing context to change the theory—is ultimately to invite control by the method and by the no-longer-examined assumptions on which it depends. It is not enough to allow history to inform the development of the theory if the theory is then treated as though it were universally applicable without periodic reexamination. All theories need to be tested and retested as circumstances change, and their basic assumptions also need to be reconsidered periodically.

Ricardo's choice to focus on distribution was also a fateful one. It distracted economists from paying attention to land, labor, and capital as such and as embedded in the natural environment. They began, instead, to think in terms of who would get the benefits of the use of each factor: to focus on landlords, laborers, and capitalists, and finally just on rent, wages, and profits. Both Ricardo and Malthus were aware of the limits that the natural world places on production, through both the law of diminishing returns in agriculture and population growth. But instead of working out an economic theory that accepts the importance of these limits and works within them, economists set out to overcome them. This in itself was not wrong, and in fact it is part of the genius of capitalism that perceived limits are constantly being overcome.

When Ricardo and Malthus were writing, in the first half of the nineteenth century, economies were still small compared to the potential resources. The problem of the scale of the economy in relation to its planetary environment would not become an issue for more than a century. So it is not at all surprising that economists, even when aware that the problem would eventually arise, concentrated on the more urgent problem before them—that of finding ways to expand economic output. Economic growth was such a new idea that *any* economic growth seemed a major accomplishment. Indeed, we might say, looking back, that it has not been until recently, in the late twentieth century, that we could be sure that economists really had solved the problem of creating economies that would grow, with ups and downs, but steadily. Every time natural limits have been reached, alternatives have been found and the economy has actually leaped forward, as happened with the shift from whale oil to petroleum in the nineteenth century, and as is happening now in a different way with the shift from copper wire to fiber optics. There can be no question that capitalism has fostered a creativity with respect to overcoming limitations that surpasses that of any culture in human history.

It is perilous, however, to neglect the difference between actually overcoming limits and ignoring them. Yes, the earth can carry far more economic activity than anyone dreamed possible in Malthus's generation. But there are still limits to how much use and waste the biosphere can take, and many scientists are telling us that we are crossing those boundaries to our peril. The circular-flow model so common in economics textbooks needs to be corrected to show the economy as a throughput system with the circular flow coming from the biosphere and returning to it (as suggested by economist Herman Daly). The long-term costs of continually running a biospheric deficit and of overloading natural systems with waste products have to be calculated. We can no longer afford to leave these issues out of economic theory and economic policy; it is neither economically efficient nor even possible to try to clean up the problems as fast as the economy produces them.

Crucial to this needed shift in economic thinking is the distinction between *overcoming* limits and *violating* them. The overcoming of limits should continue to be encouraged—indeed, we must find ways to overcome the limits of the current use of particular natural resources, such as petroleum, by substituting cleaner and more sustainable energy sources. But at the same time we have to learn to measure when we are violating limits in a manner that puts us into a dangerous deficit situation with respect to planetary systems. Producing CFCs (chlorofluorocarbons) that destroy the earth's protective ozone layer is an example of violating limits. Another is the planetwide destruction of forests that is ruining topsoil, lessening rainfall, increasing flooding, lowering oxygen levels, and causing other damage that we don't know how to measure yet. A small first step for economics would be to stop *adding* the monetary gain from such nonsustainable and destructive practices to GNP. At the micro level as well as the macro level, long-run economic viability must be *counted*, and incentives found to encourage firms to work on long-term profitability instead of short-term, one-time gain. This step would change only the accounting practices, but even that much will not be done until our thinking shifts toward supporting long-term sustainability.

John Stuart Mill contributed much that could help with this problem of distinguishing between overcoming and violating limits, and could enable economics to develop more in the direction of fostering healthy communities. Most fundamental is his view of nature as active rather than passive.[2] Viewing nature as active would change the relationship of human beings to nature and open up more possibilities of learning from, and working with, natural processes, rather than simply trying to control them.

Mill's example of Swiss agricultural communities gives us a concrete picture of how to harness individual incentives, so successful in capitalism, to work for the benefit of a community and within, rather than against, the natural setting—and all in ways that make the most of the possibilities for individual creativity in relation to the intricacies of the ecosystem people work in. Mill shows us that it *is* possible for personal self-interest and community interest to coincide, to be mutually reinforcing, *and* to provide persons with plenty to keep their interest and commitment high. A great deal could be accomplished toward transforming capitalism by following up on Mill's description of a healthy economic system by looking for, and building on, similarly healthy elements of contemporary urban and rural communities.

Unfortunately, by the time John Stuart Mill made his contribution to economics, the split between the dictates of deductive method and the realities of actual economies was too far along for Mill's excellent views of actual economies to make a real difference. In fact, Mill himself furthered the split. On the one hand he gave us the abstract ideal of *Homo economicus*, and on the other he believed that nature is active and that healthy agricultural communities are important. Then he added another split by separating the laws of production from the laws of distribution, with the result that the discussion ever since has been framed in terms of individual liberty versus social equity. In his value theory Mill assumed it was safe to emphasize individual choice because, presumably, individuals would never neglect to choose what was necessary to their basic subsistence. In this way the possibility of distinguishing in economic theory between subsistence and supplemental utility was lost. So was the possibility of distinguishing between scarcity that arises from the production side as a result of natural constraints and scarcity that arises from the demand side as a result of demand that may or may not be based on actual need. Consequently the opportunity to take into account absolute scarcity due to natural limits was also lost.

Working concepts of scarcity due to natural limits and subsistence utility based on basic human needs are two crucial concepts for a transformed economics. How to define them has to be worked out by economists in dialogue with ecologists, physicians, and anthropologists—and through broad social discourse. But if we work from an attempt to determine what are basic minimums for healthy systems, we should be able to agree on some standards.

In contrast to Mill, Marx insisted that social-equity liberalism's solution of distribution is not enough, we must deal with production. But the frustrating thing about Karl Marx is that he understood as well as John Stuart Mill the value of smaller-scale farming and manufacturing in close-knit communities—for example, the labor satisfaction of "non-alienating" work, and its beneficial effects on the long-term productivity of the soil—yet he rejected them in favor of large-scale industrialization. Marx was as thoroughly governed by his version of deductive theory as any capitalist economist has ever been, and he accepted the goal of growth along with the worst elements of industrialization. Marx recognized the destructive aspects of industrialization, but he made no attempt to find healthier ways to improve economies. In the end, Marx's "scientific impartiality" is partiality for massive production, and his use of the labor theory of value completely denies the unique contribution, or "labor," of nature, not to mention the patient, creating, labor of God.

Despite Marx's failures, he did make two crucial contributions. First and most obvious, Marx focused attention firmly on the plight of the masses of industrial workers and insisted that it is not enough to have an economy that is growing overall if the situation of those worst off is not improving. Second, his use of historical-critical methods has played an important role in the development of self-critical assessment in nearly every field. One of the areas that most needs to become more historically critical and self-critical, however, is the one Marx cared most about, economics. The economic theories of both free-market capitalism and Marxian socialism have aspired to be ranked as ahistorical science, even though physics itself is learning that objectivity and subjectivity cannot be so neatly separated.

After John Stuart Mill and Marx, deductive method took a turn toward its narrowest focus: marginal analysis as a tool for analyzing the choices of individuals in the market. This sharpest of economic tools has brought the greatest clarity yet achieved in economic theory. It is endlessly useful in market analysis and in other areas. But it has become like a fixed spotlight that illumines only one small part of the stage while much important action is going on elsewhere. Economists have fixed a great deal of attention on what marginal analysis can illuminate, with excellent results within that sphere, but at the same time they have neglected the urgent task of searching for other important knowledge. (Or, to change the metaphor, marginal analysis is the wrong tool for much urgent work, but instead of searching for better tools, economists have allowed themselves to concentrate on what the one tool of marginal analysis can do.) Even more important has been the mentality correlative to marginal analysis in the wider society that has led to a culture of crisis management and short-term responses—of responding to problems only when they become visibly urgent and acting only for short-term gain—instead of working for the long-term good.

The value theory of the marginalists was the apotheosis of hedonism and individualism: The only purpose of economic activity was thought to be the pleasurable consumption of goods by individuals (labor in this view cannot be rewarding in itself). But the problem with individual utility theory is not the hedonism, which twentieth-century economists purged from the theory. The problem is that, even though the individual is theoretically left free to choose a wider frame of values than profit maximization in the market for producers and hedonistic consumption for consumers, the system itself is designed to reinforce those goals. Producers are rewarded only for maximizing profits by means of satisfying consumers, and consumers are constantly encouraged to engage in hedonistic consumption patterns. Other values that might be defined as self-interested in a wider sense, such as making business decisions in relation to long-term profitability based on the sustainable use of resources, or refraining from high levels of consumption for the sake of health, are often detrimental to purely economic criteria, as the system has defined them, and so discouraged. With these powerful incentives, over time reality comes to look more and more like the deductive model, the ideal of *Homo economicus.*

The marginalists did understand scarcity, but once again the habit of marginal analysis and the goal of individual utility maximization led them to miss the important issue of absolute scarcity.[3] They framed their theory in a way that would encourage not conservation of scarce resources but the making scarce of abundant ones, so that their exchange value in the market would rise. While it would be beneficial to the economy as a whole over the long run to keep resources abundant, all the incentives of market capitalism are for individual firms to gain control of resources and make them scarcer for the sake of short-term profits.

Alfred Marshall was a much broader thinker than the marginalists, but as with John Stuart Mill, his use of deductive method and his quest for clarity caused a split between his theory and his analysis of economic realities. Even so, Marshall offers at least two important contributions to a transformed economics. First, he pointed out that land, though not unique from an individual point of view, *is* unique from a social perspective. Individuals can treat land like capital: it can be traded for other land or other things. But society has only a fixed amount of land and cannot trade it for other things. Nor can society substitute capital or labor for land indefinitely. Most fundamentally, only "land" (in the sense of living natural systems) can produce food.

Second, Marshall suggested another goal for the economy: Instead of growth in the production of goods, he thought economics should strive to increase growth in the "health and strength" of all the people.[4] An economics that had as its central goal the growth of healthier persons in healthier communities in healthier ecosystems would certainly encourage a different economy. Unfortunately, Marshall did not pursue this suggestion. Instead, he developed the tools of marginal analysis into the "sharp chisels" of neoclassical theory, and economics continued to pursue the dictates of the values already embedded in the method.

In the twentieth century, economics in the United States pursued the use of the tools developed in neoclassical theory to their most abstract possible forms. In the process, economics arrived at the clearest and most effective understandings of the economy yet achieved, and its basic tenets began to be applied also to the analysis of other areas of life. It became possible for the first time to examine the "macro" workings of an economy and thus for national policies to have positive effects on major problem areas such as employment, inflation, and trade.

At the same time, the process of abstraction led to the reification of material life in terms of "money": land, labor, and capital came to be treated more and more as if they were the same and interchangeable; profit maximization led to an emphasis on the short term even when long-run profits could be higher; and the whole society was directed more and more by massive government interventions through monetary manipulations. Both social-equity liberalism (represented by John Maynard Keynes) and laissez-faire liberalism (represented by Milton Friedman) were affected by this process of abstraction.

The atomistic individualism of Newtonian mechanics also reached its ultimate social forms in the economy: mediating communities dropped out of the picture, leaving individuals (all alike and interchangeable) as statistical averages in macroaggregations. Neither capitalism nor Marxian socialism paid attention to communities as such; both called for ready transfer of labor and capital investment for the sake of economic efficiency, with little regard for the social inefficiency of constant community disruption.

None of this abstracting and individualizing trend was peculiar to economics. Every area of U.S. culture was affected, and every academic discipline has tended in the same directions. At the same time that economics was discovering marginal analysis and becoming intent on the choices of individuals in the market, theology was also focusing on individual choice. Both conservative evangelicals and liberal existentialists emphasized the decisions of individuals about their faith. But no discipline has been more effective than economics in influencing the whole society.

In sum, in the twentieth-century neoclassical economic theory emerged with the claim to be a scientific and value-free discipline. While the successes of capitalist economies, which neoclassical theory strives to describe and support, have been tremendous, it is time for economics to move on and take into account much more fundamentally the developments of the past century. Economic theory needs to become more historical, acknowledge and debate its own embedded and assumed values, and pay more attention to major contextual changes. While this debate is under way, it is urgent that the changes this reassessment entails be brought into basic economics texts and into the practices of the discipline with respect to economic policy recommendations. Other disciplines, including the sciences, need to do the same, but it is especially important that economics do so because of its enormous impact on society.

FOUNDATIONS FOR TRANSFORMING ECONOMICS

Health Instead of Wealth

Two centuries ago Western societies set out to increase wealth. They have succeeded, but it is increasingly evident that the success of capitalism cannot be sustained as is. The ever increasing production of consumer goods and services cannot remain *the* central goal of economies—the biosphere simply cannot handle it. This does *not* mean that economies should not increase their production of goods where appropriate. But this should not be the driving purpose. My proposal is to take up Alfred Marshall's call to change our social-economic goal from growth in production to growth in "health and strength." Adam Smith inquired into the "nature and causes of the wealth of nations." I suggest we inquire into the nature and causes of the health of communities, both human and natural, and apply what is being learned about health to transform economics.[5]

Much that will be useful to economics has already been learned. Medicine, biology, ecology, anthropology, physics, and many other areas of knowledge have advanced rapidly and have a great deal to offer to the transformation of economics. One advantage of using "health" as the central goal of economics is the fact that it is a concept amenable to quantifiable measures as well as qualitative ones. Neoclassical economists find it difficult to discuss what could be a "good" economics or a "good" community, since they assume that what is good can be defined only by each individual for himself or herself. But health is firmly rooted in physical categories that do have objective as well as subjective aspects. The objective dimensions of health are amenable to quantifiable measures that could be used in economic statistics to assess economic success. For example, we know how many calories per day people need for basic physical health. Per capita calorie consumption, along with other appropriate measures of material life, could be used to compare subsistence economies with market economies in Third World countries, to find out how successful they are at the most basic level.

It is also possible to devise indicators of the overall health of communities and the most vulnerable within them, as well as to use indicators of individual health. The quality of the community water supply, the number of small businesses, the quality of the educational system, the level of participation in community activities (for example, volunteer activities, religious organizations, the arts, local sports, voting levels), and whether the local economy is diversified enough to manage economic downturns—all these are indicators of community health, including economic health. We know that healthy persons require a variety of foods, shelter, and clothing suited to local conditions, as well as certain basic freedoms, rights, and the ability to participate in community life. Insofar as these basics are also amenable to measurement, they should be built into statistics about basic needs—indeed, this is already being done in social-indicator statistics, but it could be done more in relation to economic indicators as well.

Clearly, economics would be transformed if health rather than wealth were the goal of societies (or, even better, healthy communities rather than wealthy individuals). All social and economic activities would be scrutinized for their efficiency in promoting healthy communities rather than simply generating wealth. This would not mean that wealth would disappear. Economics would still be about that area of human activity that deals with material life. And no doubt many of the basic tenets of capitalism would remain, since they have proven durable, creative, and effective.

Foremost is the principle that distant, centralized decision making is clumsy, inefficient, and often unjust. But this is true for *all* kinds of decisions, whether it is government or industry that is making them. Luckily the movement to decentralize decision making is already under way and spreading rapidly, precisely because even the most top-heavy of big corporations, such as General Motors, are realizing that Adam Smith was right: local people in their local situations do usually know what needs to be done on the spot and can do it quickly. Consequently both businesses and governments are learning to give more responsibility and control to those who know best what to do with it. This does not mean that *all* decisions should be made locally. The need for coordination at levels beyond the local will always exist. A useful principle to follow is the old Catholic doctrine of "subsidiarity"—the principle that higher organizations exist to serve lower ones and should perform only those functions that the more basic units of society (or social organizations) cannot perform for themselves.

An economics with a central goal of health would pay attention to emerging discussions of what constitutes a healthy community and would seek to develop methods contributing to that goal. Value theory would be recast. At the very least, individual utility theory would be placed firmly in a wider context of values that would include recognition of intrinsic value and inherent relations, and use value as well as exchange value.[6] Economists would likely try to find ways to distinguish between subsistence utility and supplemental utility, and sustainable use versus permanent depletion, so that economies could be assessed on whether they have promoted the basic health of all for the long term. Instead of GNP, economists would develop measures of economic welfare like the ISEW (Index of Sustainable Economic Welfare) that take into account measures of personal and community health such as sustainable use of resources and whether the need for police services was increasing or decreasing. One effective place to begin would be to insist that economic measures take into account long-term gains and losses instead of just measuring short-term profits, so that the real economic costs of nonsustainable uses of resources show up.

Methods That Are Historical/Critical and Inductive as well as Deductive

Economics needs to return to its classical roots and, like all the disciplines, needs to retreat from the high level of abstraction that has removed it so far from the real issues of material life. The basic assumptions embedded in the deductive model of neoclassical economics have not been revised for over two hundred years, and evidence is piling up that they need to be. Luckily, the resources needed are becoming available. The mechanistic model of Newton has been surpassed by physics, and the anthropology of atomistic individualism based on it has also been surpassed. Economic theory would be radically improved if it modeled itself more on contemporary physics (or, even better, on biology and ecology), and adopted a more adequate anthropology.

Deductive method has proven to be powerful and important, especially where the full reality is so messy. Inductive methods alone can be just as ahistorical, and just as prone to be shaped by the subjective views of researchers as are deductive methods. So both methods need to be subjected to historical-critical scrutiny. Economic theorems that were developed in one historical context, such as the theory of comparative advantage, must be periodically reassessed to see if the conditions that made them valid still hold. Deductive methods will still be used, but the deductive model of neoclassical economics needs to be transformed in itself and related closely to historical criticism and inductive research.

The tools used by researchers must also be kept firmly in their proper places and not allowed to determine what researchers will work on. Research should focus on what needs to be learned and ways developed to accomplish that, not on what the tools already at hand can do. In the twentieth century economics was dominated by economists who mostly worked on what the tools developed decades before could do. There were few economic theorists like those of the nineteenth century, who worked to assess the methods and basic issues of economic theory, let alone the foundational assumptions. There have been no truly foundational changes in economics in over a century. It may be no accident that, except for Ricardo, all the major economists who contributed to major changes—Smith, Malthus, Mill, Marx, Marshall, and Keynes—were trained in philosophy and/or theology. An economic theory that served an economics for healthy communities would be based in a different anthropology and a different physics and metaphysics.

Homo Salutaris *Instead of* Homo Economicus

As we have seen, John Stuart Mill's *Homo economicus* functioned as a basic premise for deductive theory and became an ideal for economics that eventually had a strong impact on the culture. If we must use such simple images to orient our discussions about economics, I propose *Homo salutaris* as a much better candidate. The "healthy human" at least moves the center of attention from a narrow range of individual economic activity to the question of what makes for healthy human beings. That would open up the imagination of economists to take into account a wider range of issues that are important to the arrangement of material life.

The concept of *Homo economicus* truncated radically the understanding of human persons by focusing narrowly on the single motive of wealth maximizing at the expense of other important values and relations. This made it possible to pit the goals of economic activity against each other, so that family and community values became incompatible with profit-making values. When pursued as an ideal, *Homo economicus* narrows the person to a "rational" utility-maximizing individual. The idea of *Homo salutaris*, by contrast, widens the understanding. When developed as an ideal for human persons, it quickly becomes obvious that individuals cannot be healthy unless they have healthy relationships with others in healthy communities in healthy ecosystems.

The anthropology that I would recommend for a transformed economics is one that moves beyond the polarized choices of atomistic individualism versus functionalistic sociology. In individualism relationships are assumed to be voluntary and external to individual identity. In functional anthropologies (including some forms of communism), the person is subsumed into the society, and individual identity is denied. We have been forced to choose between being unrelated or dissolved—human beings as billiard balls or as cogs in the machinery of the state. But *Homo salutaris* needs both individuality *and* social relations. Neither freedom nor justice can be achieved without both. An anthropology of "persons-in-community" like that proposed by Daly and Cobb would provide the needed foundation. Daly and Cobb argue that we "come into being in and through relationships and have no identity apart from them."[7] We are more than those relationships, but "what more we are also depends on the character of these societies."[8] Because of this constitutive relationality, human individuality itself requires social relations to develop. Human persons can be healthy only in the context of a network of basically healthy relations that includes families related to communities related to the ecosystems in which they exist. Economics would be placed within these nested sets of relations.

Instead of individual utility, the material life of communities and what makes them healthier would receive the sustained attention of economics. Criteria for this would have to be worked out, of course, but we already have some clues. We know that there is no one standard for healthy communities, and that very diverse communities can be healthy—and in fact, since community health depends on adapting to local ecosystems, we know that lack of diversity between communities would be an unhealthy sign. The same is true of diversity within communities: While there may be some very homogeneous communities that are relatively healthy, there must be *some* diversity, or the community will be unable to adapt to changing social and economic conditions. And it seems clear that the healthier the community, the more diversity it can tolerate and even use constructively. Appropriate levels of individual and collaborative creativity and participation need to be fostered; and some communities will be known for great music while others for great technology.

It seems clear that overall, the worldwide trend toward rural depopulation and urban overpopulation has gone too far, and rural communities must be revitalized. I do *not* mean to idealize rural communities and denigrate urban centers. While it is important to find a healthier balance between cities and small towns, it is just as crucial to work on cultivating healthy urban communities as rural ones. And despite disintegration in urban areas, there are still many healthy urban neighborhoods in many great cities from which much can be learned.

This anthropology does not assume that human beings are sinless and that perfect freedom and justice are possible in human economies and societies. Just the opposite. It is unhealthy to pretend that perfection is possible and perfect harmony attainable. But it is quite possible to distinguish between healthy and unhealthy conflict, and between healthy and destructive competition. It is also commonly understood that health is not an either/or state but a spectrum along which it is possible to be getting healthier or getting sicker. Everyone knows that a broken bone heals but is never quite the same. And it is possible to be relatively healthy in old age and to deal with disabilities in healthy or unhealthy ways. It should be possible to devise ways of measuring whether communities are getting healthier or sicker for economic systems to take account of.

Nor would I presume to assume that the concept of *Homo salutaris*, and the quest for healthy human and natural communities, would not develop its own dangers and ways of becoming problematic. Evil will show up whatever we do. It would be important, for instance, to work hard to avoid falling into a kind of tyranny of health—the sort that was fostered in Nazi Germany. It would be a terrible tragedy if in the name of "health" we chose one physical type to idealize at the expense of all others. A cult of "health" might also try to deny that death and disease are natural and necessary parts of life. But I am confident that if we continue to turn to nature to learn what is healthy, and continually reexamine our basic assumptions and values, we will be less prone to fall into these traps.

The anthropology of *persons-in-community* provides a context in which some of the most persistently difficult dualisms of the modern debate will be overcome. We have already noted how the gulf between individual and society is bridged. Closely related to this is the split in liberalism between those who see justice in terms of individual freedom and those who see it in terms of social equity. Personal freedom requires both possibilities for independent action and opportunities for cooperative contributions and participation. Even Mozart could not have achieved the heights of his individual musical genius without the support and openness of his society to his work. On the other side, social health requires the maximization of opportunities for all of society's members in order to make the fullest possible use of their gifts and talents. Social equity without personal freedom is quickly reduced to a lowest common denominator—as in the colorless, deadening sameness of East European socialism. But individual freedom without social equity is highly inefficient for social health, since those left on the margins are unable to make their contributions to the whole. The concept of participation is needed to connect individual liberty and social equity and move beyond the false choices they set up.

In economics the split between micro and macro might also be overcome by the reintroduction of mediating levels between the two arenas. Instead of individual firms interacting at the micro level and giant aggregates at the macro level, economic theory will be able to take into account the mediating interactions that go on between the two levels by taking local and regional economies and their communities into account.

Living Natural Systems Instead of the Mechanical Model

One irony of neoclassical economics is that, while it exalts individual human freedom, it is based on a physics that denies freedom in the natural world. Because human beings are part of the natural world, it is impossible to maintain a split between a deterministic nature and a free humanity. And, indeed, the mechanistic worldview is constantly undermining the very freedom that economists want to promote. We need to return to the original instinct of the Physiocrats and look to living systems for wisdom about how to arrange economies.

In one way the Physiocrats were correct to maintain that all economic "gain" comes from agriculture: It is true that the planet's only outside source of energy is sunlight, and it is still true that plants garner that sunlight and turn it into usable material more efficiently than anything else. Strictly speaking, the harvesting of plants *is* by far the major source of real matter and energy gain in the economy. Virtually everything else is, as John Stuart Mill pointed out, moving natural resources around and changing them to make them useful to human beings. Nature *is* actively producing everything human beings use. Exchange value may be added in manufacturing, but some energy, resources, capital, and labor are lost. Newton's law of entropy is as important as Quesnay's idea about net product. Measures of economic efficiency should be redesigned to take this into account—especially actual (not subsidized) energy costs. Such a redesign would dramatically alter the perception of efficiency. For example, U.S. agriculture, often touted as a model of efficiency, turns out to be one of the least efficient modes of food production in the world.

Land (including all of nonhuman nature) needs to be restored in economic theory as a unique factor that cannot be treated in terms of either capital (capitalism) or labor (Marxism). It would be more accurate to treat both capital and labor as forms of land—as based in the natural world. To make land the prior and most fundamental factor would, like the notion of *Homo salutaris*, widen the scope of economics instead of narrowing it. And to treat human beings and human-developed capital as part of nature would surely have far healthier consequences than the current tendency to treat nature and human beings as forms of capital. But at the very least, land must be given unique and equal status so that, as Alfred Marshall said, the three factors of production hold each other up like three pieces of fruit in a bowl.

Classical economics picked up on "the circulation of the blood" as a metaphor useful for analyzing the circular flow of production and consumption, and this model is still taught in introductory economics textbooks.[9] Some current textbooks have improved greatly on this in the past ten years, by adding resource and product markets to the circular flow, but they still do not make clear that production and consumption work in throughput fashion, with the flow going from the natural sources of resources and back to the natural systems that must take in the generated waste. When the long-term economic costs of resource depletion and waste management are not included, the economic calculations of what goods and services really cost are not accurate. This is of course financially advantageous for individual firms, but it is economically and socially disastrous for communities. As we have seen, waiting for market prices to rise before dealing with resource damage may be financially beneficial to some, but it is economically damaging to all in the long run because the resource base that all depend on is diminished. Treating production and consumption as throughput in a biologically based circular system would help to correct these problems and shift economies toward sustainable use and the conservation of the ecosystems on which they depend.

Economics can learn many other things from ecosystems that will help correct the comparatively clumsy and often destructive consequences of the mechanical model. Fortunately, the business world is not waiting for economic theory to change. There is a strong movement in business to become more like living ecosystems and less like machines. For example, the era of interchangeable parts and cookie-cutter products is nearly over—product differentiation to find diverse market niches is well under way. The practice of treating laborers as interchangeable parts is also ending. Instead, workers are being trained to work as teams that have high levels of responsibility for their work, and much more room for creativity.[10] Biologists have been teaching that the "survival of the fittest" is wrong; a better way to put it is the "survival of those who find a niche in which to fit." Corporations are also discovering that diversity is crucial for survival—diversity not only of products but also of ideas. All of these new ways of arranging economic life also have the advantage of broadening opportunities for meaningful participation for people in society through their work and the way they work. We are moving beyond the narrow conception that work is solely for the purpose of consumption, and the creativity fostered so well by capitalism is helping with this task.

FOUNDATIONS FOR TRANSFORMING THE CULTURE

Theological and Philosophical Issues

Free-market capitalism and Marxian socialism did not develop in a cultural vacuum. They depend on ideas that permeate Western culture and that have developed over centuries. In order to transform economics, it is necessary also to change the culture in which material life is lived. Philosophy and theology have important roles in this, as they did in the shaping of the modern era that in turn has shaped economics. Nor have philosophy and theology been innocent of the kinds of problems that we have seen in economic history and theory. They too need to be transformed by an anthropology of *persons-in-community* and a worldview based more in living natural systems than Newtonian mechanics.

Relations as Internal and Implications for Freedom and Justice

Free-market capitalism takes for granted a background of the philosophical and theological nominalism/voluntarism that pervades not only economics but Western culture, especially U.S. culture. This is the underlying reason that the Enlightenment philosophers and their laissez-faire counterparts understood natural law so differently from the Roman Catholic tradition. In the Aristotelian-Thomistic framework, it is "natural" for persons to fit into their place in the hierarchy, as everything is fixed in creation by God. But in the nominalist-voluntarist scheme, where nothing is inherently related to anything else, it is "natural" for entities to bounce around at liberty, controlled only by externally imposed "laws."

This may help explain why liberals of both kinds tend to conceive of law only in terms of external coercion rather than as internally effected through mediating relations. It may also account for the extreme need in modern culture to control nature. Since God can no longer be counted on to keep everything in its place (as Newton believed), human beings have to do it.

This view of relations as external to unrelated substances also underlies the way modern economies, both capitalist and Marxist, have not hesitated to move both human beings and natural resources about to suit the needs of industrialization. Communities and natural ecosystems have no importance in their own right.

Philosophy and theology that can undergird a transformed economics for healthy persons-in-community are already available, especially in the work of Alfred North Whitehead and the process/relational movement. Process thought provides a worldview more related to developments in contemporary physics than Newtonian mechanics, based on the premise that all entities are internally as well as externally related. Instead of the "substance" thinking that underlies the opposing views of determinism and voluntarism (and makes it difficult to find an alternative to both), process thought asserts that the universe consists of events, not substances. In this view, there are no "things"—no "atoms" bouncing around wholly independent of context and no "chain of being" that holds everything in place. Instead, there are only events that are all internally related to all other events, so that no entity is wholly independent or wholly dependent. Rather, *all* entities have inheritances from the past that provide the context for both the amount of determination they receive and the range of freedom they have available to them.

In this view human beings may have more personal freedom than any other entities, but they are not different in kind from everything else. The natural world is not wholly deterministic and human beings are not wholly free, as neoclassical economics has assumed, along with most of modern philosophy. Both freedom and determination are mediated by relations, and this is the reason why human beings need freedom to contribute their uniqueness to others just as much as they need freedom to become unique.

This means that *both* the laissez-faire liberals who view justice in terms of individual liberty *and* the social-equity liberals who view justice in terms of social equity are right. But both are missing the mediation of relations in communities. Justice is not simply a matter of rendering to each his or her due in an individualistic fashion. Justice is a matter of healthy relations in which both freedom from coercion and freedom for contribution and participation (and therefore some access to livelihood or some meaningful role in society) are available for all persons in their communities.

We may be able to move beyond the impasse between social equity and individual liberty if we examine economies and societies from the perspective of the kind of participation they encourage. From this perspective, neither capitalist nor Marxist societies have done well at optimizing participation. Capitalist societies do encourage high creativity and innovation but also tend to have high rates of unemployment in which effective participation is denied altogether. The high value placed on consumption has also fostered passive forms of entertainment—from watching sports to listening to music—that have undermined direct participation by masses of people in favor of high achievement and creativity by a few. Marxist societies seemed to achieve fuller employment, but were plagued by low levels of creativity and innovation because of the lack of personal investment on the part of most people.

Intrinsic Value and the Doctrine of God

Voluntarism is characterized first and foremost by its emphasis on freedom of choice. Originally voluntarism was discussed in terms of the absolute freedom of God to do exactly as God pleases. The doctrine insisted that whatever God chooses must be good, simply because God chose it. This was a powerful impetus to thinking of value solely in terms of subjective choice in general.

Eventually, value as dependent solely on individual choice was applied to human choices and enshrined in Western culture most powerfully through individual utility theory in neoclassical economics.

As we have seen, the power of this doctrine has been so great that it has become very difficult to talk about *any* comparison of value—even between two persons, let alone the "common good" of a community. Natural communities have suffered even more, since nonhuman creatures are accorded no intrinsic value at all and are treated solely as resources for human use. (Humans are still assigned intrinsic value as a leftover from the doctrine that human beings carry the "image of God," though there is little in secular culture to protect this value.)

As long as value is believed to be wholly subjective, human rights are a matter of social whim, and human and natural communities cannot be defended. But both process thought and the biblical tradition, as well as most other religious traditions, deny that subjective value is the only or most important form of value. Instead, these traditions affirm that simply to exist is to have intrinsic value. Once any entity comes into existence, the value realized in the entity is inherent in it and not a function of anyone else's valuation, even God's. To exist is to be a realization of some measure of concrete value, and it is the discovery and recognition of this value that provides the foundation for human rights and the right of other creatures to exist in healthy natural ecosystems.

Recognition of intrinsic value does not imply according "equal rights" to all entities, even if that were possible, which it obviously is not. In any case, that is an individualistic notion. But it does imply that human beings do not have the right so to disrupt ecosystems that other species are destroyed. Because all creatures are internally related, human beings need to share the planet with other human and nonhuman creatures in the context of healthy ecosystems. Because all creatures have intrinsic value, other creatures also have the *right* to their natural existence. This provides a philosophical and ethical framework to undergird an economics for health that will work to achieve a sustainable use of resources that respects species diversity so that all creatures can flourish together.

But we still have not dealt with the source of the problem—the doctrine of God that teaches that value is solely subjective and arbitrary (and that views God that way as well: as arbitrary judge). This view of God has already been changing in the culture, and many now reject this image of God in favor of understanding God as a loving parent who steadfastly cares for the whole of creation. This latter view has been developed in process thought and is congruent with the biblical tradition as well, where creation is fully included in salvation and redemption.[11]

Much remains to be done. The confusion about natural law needs to be dealt with in philosophy and theology, and a version of natural law theory developed that reconciles internal relations with freedom. In economics the transformation of capitalism and economic theory is overdue. Two hundred years ago Adam Smith and his Enlightenment colleagues set out to transform the mercantilism and political oligarchies of their day into a more open, democratic, and participatory political and economic system. If they could do it, we can. This volume is a contribution to that process of transformation.

Notes

INTRODUCTION: THE CHOICES FOR WEALTH OVER HEALTH OF NATIONS

1. See Peter L. Berger, *Pyramids of Sacrifice* (New York: Basic Books, 1974), and *The Capitalist Revolution* (New York: Basic Books, 1987). Also Michael Novak, *The Spirit of Democratic Capitalism* (New York: Simon & Schuster, 1982).

2. John Neville Keynes, "The Scope and Method of Political Economy" (1917). Reprinted in *The Philosophy of Economics: An Anthology*, ed. Daniel M. Hausman (Cambridge: Cambridge University Press, 1984), 76.

3. I use *land* and *nature* interchangeably, since land is the term used in economics to designate everything nature provides.

4. See Stephen C. Munday, *Current Developments in Economics* (New York: St. Martin's Press, 1996), 4 and 16. In recent years many more economists have begun working on environmental issues, and the Institutionalists and neo-Institutionalists have always paid more attention to the impact of economics on communities. See recent issues of the *American Economic Review*, the *Journal of Economics and Sociology*, the *Journal of Economic Issues*, and *Ecological Economics*. As yet, however, mainstream neoclassical theory still dominates and has not been internally transformed. See Nahid Aslanbeigui and Michele I. Naples, eds., *Rethinking Economic Principles: Critical Essays on Introductory Textbooks* (Chicago: Richard D. Irwin, 1996), vol. 2, 12–15, 198–99.

5. Most interdisciplinary work typically brings together insights from different disciplines, but accepts the basic assumptions of each discipline as given. My argument is that a fresh examination of the basic assumptions and foundational values of each discipline in itself and in relation to other arenas of knowledge and experience is overdue in all the disciplines.

6. See Herman E. Daly and John B. Cobb Jr., *For the Common Good: Redirecting the Economy Toward Community, the Environment, and a Sustainable Future* (Boston: Beacon Press, 1989).

1. FOR ECONOMIC GROWTH AND INDIVIDUALISM OVER THE LAND

1. Marquis de Mirabeau, *Correspondance Générale de J. J. Rousseau*, ed. T. Dufour, vol. 17 (1932), 171–72. In Ronald L. Meek, *The Economics of Physiocracy: Essays and Translations* (Cambridge: Harvard University Press, 1963), 19–20.

2. François Quesnay, "Corn," trans. from the text as reproduced in *François Quesnay et la Physiocratie* (Paris: *Institut National d'Etudes Démographiques*, 1958), vol. 2, 495–510. In Meek, *The Economics of Physiocracy*, 73.

3. John Locke, *Two Treatises of Civil Government* (London: J. M. Dent & Sons, 1924), 137.

4. Adam Smith, *An Inquiry into the Nature and Causes of the Wealth of Nations* (1776), ed. Edwin Cannan (New York: Modern Library, 1937), vol. 2, 32.

5. There are some who agree with him, and even argue that trade was not as important as agriculture to economic development, even in England. See Paul Bairoch, *Cities and Economic Development: From the Dawn of History to the Present* (Chicago: University of Chicago Press, 1988), 246.

6. Smith, *Wealth of Nations*, vol. 1, 344.

7. Ibid., 348.

8. Ibid.

9. Ibid., 356–57.

10. Ibid., 357.

11. Ibid., 420.

12. See John P. Lewis and Valeriana Kallab, eds., *Development Strategies Reconsidered* (New Brunswick, N.J.: Transaction Books, 1986), 5–10. These "mainstream" (their term) development analysts make this comment about development and agriculture: "We wonder whether a standardized prescription of export-led growth will meet the needs of big low-income countries in the latter 1980s as well as it did those of small and medium size middle-income countries in the 1960s and 1970s. . . . We have a sense that . . . the relationship of agriculture and industry never got adequately sorted out—nor, more recently, has the balance to be sought between export expansion and some version of internal agro-industrial expansion as engines of growth" (p. 10).

13. Peter L. Berger, *The Capitalist Revolution* (New York: Basic Books, 1986), ch. 7, "East Asian Capitalism."

14. Henry Higgs, *The Physiocrats: Six Lectures on the French Economistes of the Eighteenth Century* (New York: Langland Press, 1952), 92. See also Elizabeth Fox-Genovese, *The Origins of Physiocracy: Economic Revolution and Social Order in Eighteenth Century France* (Ithaca, N.Y.: Cornell University Press, 1976), 28.

15. Smith, *Wealth of Nations*, vol. 1, 2.
16. Ibid., 6–7.
17. Ibid., 32.
18. Ibid., 2.
19. Berger, *Capitalist Revolution*, 44.
20. Ibid., 43–44.
21. Marvin Harris, "Murders in Eden," in *Anthropology: Contemporary Perspectives*, ed. David E. K. Hunter and Phillip Whitten (Boston: Little, Brown, 1985), 196–97.
22. Harris, "Murders in Eden," 196–97.
23. Smith, *Wealth of Nations*, vol 2, 267.
24. See William Ferguson, *Scotland: 1689 to the Present, vol. 4, The Edinburgh History of Scotland* (Edinburgh: Mercat Press, 1987), 167; and Susan Parman, *Scottish Crofters* (Fort Worth: Holt, Rinehart & Winston, 1990), 32.
25. Smith, *Wealth of Nations*, vol 1, 80.
26. T. C. Smout, *A Century of the Scottish People: 1830–1950* (New Haven, Conn.: Yale University Press, 1986), 66.
27. Smout, *Scottish People*, 66–67.
28. To understand Smith fully it is necessary to read *Wealth of Nations* in relation to *Moral Sentiments;* unfortunately, the latter book has had little impact compared to that of *Wealth of Nations*, and the individualism in *Wealth of Nations* has consequently been read in abstraction from social relations. Because *Wealth of Nations*, and not *Moral Sentiments*, influenced the development of economics, we will concentrate on what Smith says in *Wealth of Nations*.
29. Smith, *Wealth of Nations*, vol. 1, 17–18.
30. Ibid., 393.
31. Ibid., 421–22.
32. Ibid., 421.
33. Ibid.
34. See, e.g., Stephen C. R. Munday, *Current Developments in Economics* (New York: St. Martin's Press, 1996), 17; and John B. Taylor, *Economics* (Boston: Houghton Mifflin, 1995), 25.
35. Smith, *Wealth of Nations*, vol. 1, 131.
36. Richard G. Lipsey, Peter O. Steiner, Douglas D. Purvis, and Paul N. Courant, *Economics*, 9th ed. (New York: Harper & Row, 1990), 46.
37. This phrase was used by James Kuhn, dean of Columbia University Business School, in a discussion of this point at the Colloquium on Reformed Faith and Economics, Ghost Ranch, New Mexico, August 1985.
38. See, e.g., Lipsey et al., *Economics*, 48.

2. FOR DEDUCTIVE METHOD AND RENT OVER POOR RELIEF

1. David Ricardo, *The Principles of Political Economy and Taxation* (1817) (London: Dent, 1965), 82–87.
2. Ibid., 80.
3. Ibid., 83.
4. See Alan B. Krueger, "The Truth about Wages," *New York Times*, July 31, 1997, A17; and Ford Foundation Project on Social Welfare and the American Future, *The Common Good: Social Welfare and the American Future: Policy Recommendations of the Executive Panel* (New York: Ford Foundation, 1989), 51.
5. See Herman E. Daly and John B. Cobb Jr., *For the Common Good: Redirecting the Economy toward Community, the Environment, and a Sustainable Future* (Boston: Beacon Press, 1989), ch. 11, 209–18.
6. Ricardo, *Principles*, 83.
7. Thomas Malthus, *Principles of Political Economy* (1836) (Clifton, N.J.: Augustus M. Kelley, 1974), 4, 5, 6.
8. Ingrid Hahne Rima, *Development of Economic Analysis* (Homewood, Ill.: Richard D. Irwin, 1978), 104; and Ronald L. Meek, ed., *Marx and Engels on Malthus*, trans. Dorothea L. Meek and Ronald L. Meek (New York: International Publishers, 1954), 116–17.
9. Ricardo, *Principles*, 1.
10. Malthus, *Principles*, 8–9.
11. Ricardo, *Principles*, 6.
12. According to Peter Mathias, only "half the cultivated land of England was enclosed before the 18th century began. . . . Only 130 Parliamentary Enclosure Acts were on the statute book before 1760. One thousand were then passed during the next 40 years." Peter Mathias, "Agriculture and Industrialization," *The First Industrial Revolutions*, ed. Peter Mathias and John A. Davis (Oxford: Basil Blackwell, 1989), 102.
13. Christopher Hill, *Change and Continuity in 17th Century England* (Cambridge: Harvard University Press, 1975), 236.
14. Ricardo, *Principles*, 33.
15. Ibid.
16. Ibid., 37.
17. Ibid., 38.
18. Ibid., 182
19. Ibid., 191.
20. Ibid., 184–85.
21. Ibid., 71.
22. Ibid., 71–76.
23. See Ricardo, *Principles*, 33, 38, 39, and especially 189–91. George Stigler

claims that Ricardo includes the value of capital as well as labor in exchange value, though the value of capital is much less (*Essays in the History of Economics* [Chicago: University of Chicago Press, 1965], 191.) If Ricardo does do this, he does not do so in his statements about his theory, as we saw above in his comments on Say's misunderstanding of Smith. There, capital and land add to wealth, but not to exchange value. In any case, whether Ricardo included capital in some fashion in exchange value or not, he definitely ruled out land.

24. Ricardo's footnote: "*Elemens d'Ideologie,* vol. iv, p. 99."
25. Ricardo, *Principles,* 189–90.
26. Malthus, *Principles,* 141.
27. Ibid.
28. Ibid., 195.
29. Ibid.
30. Ibid., 146.
31. Ibid., 142–43.
32. Ibid., 107–8.
33. Ibid., 106, note.
34. See Rima, *Economic Analysis,* 118.
35. See, e.g., Karl Marx, *Theories of Surplus Value,* vol. 2: "Malthus . . . like a true member of the English State Church, . . . was a professional sycophant of the landed aristocracy, whose rents, sinecures, extravagance, heartlessness, etc., he justified from the economic point of view." In Meek, *Marx and Engels on Malthus,* 116–17.

3. FOR MAXIMIZING WEALTH OVER SOCIAL REDISTRIBUTION

1. John Stuart Mill, "On the Definition and Method of Political Economy," *The Philosophy of Economics,* ed. Daniel M. Hausman (Cambridge: Cambridge University Press, 1984), 52–53.
2. Mill, "On the Definition and Method of Political Economy," 52–53.
3. Ibid., 57.
4. John Stuart Mill, *Principles of Political Economy* (1848), ed. William Ashley (Clifton, N.J.: Augustus M. Kelley, 1973), 23–25.
5. Ibid., 26.
6. Ibid., 176.
7. Ibid.
8. Ibid., 177.
9. Ibid., 187.
10. Mill's footnote: "M. de Sismondi, *Etudes sur l'Economie Politique,* Essai III," *Principles,* 258–60.
11. Mill, *Principles,* 264.

12. Ibid., 285–86.
13. Marty Strange, *Family Farming: A New Economic Vision* (Lincoln: University of Nebraska Press, 1988), 86–87, with reference to the classic study by Walter Goldschmidt, *As You Sow: Three Studies in the Social Consequences of Agribusiness* (Montclair, N.J.: Allanheld, Osmun, 1947).
14. Strange, *Family Farming*, 204–5.
15. Wendell Berry, *The Unsettling of America: Culture and Agriculture* (San Francisco: Sierra Club Books, 1977), 11.
16. Mill, *Principles*, 45.
17. Ibid.
18. Ibid., 49.
19. Ibid., 54.
20. Ibid., 67.
21. Ibid., 66–67.
22. Ibid., 68.
23. Ibid.
24. Ibid., 199.
25. Ibid., 199–200.
26. Ibid., 176.
27. Ibid., 200.
28. John Stuart Mill, *On Liberty* (Boston: Ticknor and Fields, 1863), 29.
29. Ibid., 748–49.
30. Ibid., 750.
31. Ibid.
32. Ibid., 457.
33. Ibid., 467–68.
34. Ibid., 468.
35. Ibid., 472.
36. Ibid., 442.
37. Ibid., 447.

4. FOR HISTORY AND INDUSTRIALIZATION OVER RURAL LIFE

1. "Highland clearances" refers to the process of "clearing" Scottish land of the resident peasants. Marx describes how land that had been held in common for centuries was converted into private property by the nobility and then gradually shifted to forms of agriculture more profitable to them, which resulted in the creation of a "surplus" of people who formerly had fed themselves on their own lands. The process was sped by the politics of the Jacobite rebellion of the 1700s: it was another way to punish the Highlanders who had supported "Bonnie Prince Charlie" in his futile attempt to gain the throne. Marx writes that "in the 18th century the hunted-out

Gaels were forbidden to emigrate from the country, with a view to driving them by force to Glasgow and other manufacturing towns" (Karl Marx, *Capital* [New York: Modern Library, 1906], p. 801.). The clearances went on into the nineteenth century, and the population of the Highlands has never recovered. Marx cites the example of Duchess Sutherland, who decided to turn the whole 794,000 acres of the Sutherland clan into a sheep-walk, and so from 1814 to 1820 evicted all 15,000 Sutherlands who were left from earlier clearances (p. 802).

2. Karl Marx, *Theories of Surplus Value* (1861–63), English edition 1952, in Ronald L. Meek, ed., *Marx and Engels on Malthus*, trans. Dorothea L. Meek and Ronald L. Meek (New York: International Publishers, 1954), 116–17.
3. Ibid., 119.
4. Ibid.
5. Ibid., 120.
6. Ibid., 121.
7. Peter L. Berger, *Pyramids of Sacrifice* (New York: Basic Books, 1974), 139.
8. Karl Marx, *Capital*, ed. Frederick Engels and trans. of 3d German edition by Samuel Moore and Edward Aveling (New York: Modern Library, 1906), 41.
9. Ibid., 42.
10. Ibid., 43.
11. Ibid., 44.
12. Ibid., 45.
13. Ibid., 47.
14. Ibid.
15. Ibid., 50.
16. Ibid., 47.
17. Ibid., 94.
18. Ernest Mandel, *An Introduction to Marxist Economic Theory* (New York: Pathfinder Press, 1970), 25–28.
19. Marx, *Capital*, 81
20. Karl Marx and Friedrich Engels, *The German Ideology* (1845–46), excerpts from Part 1, in John E. Elliott, *Marx and Engels on Economics, Politics, and Society: Essential Readings with Editorial Commentary* (Santa Monica, Cal.: Goodyear Publishing, 1981), 5.
21. Marx and Engels, *The German Ideology*, 7.
22. Karl Marx, *Grundrisse: Foundations of the Critique of Political Economy*, trans. Martin Nicolaus (New York: Random House, 1973). In *The Philosophy of Economics*, ed. Daniel M. Hausman (Cambridge: Cambridge University Press, 1984), 149–50.
23. Marx, *Capital*, 91–92.
24. Ibid., 204.
25. Ibid., 205.

26. Ibid., 422–23.
27. Karl Marx and Friedrich Engels, *Manifesto of the Communist Party* (1848), ed. Friedrich Engels and trans. Samuel Moore (New York: International Publishers, 1932), reprinted in *Marx on Economics*, ed. Robert Freedman (New York: Harcourt, Brace & World, 1961), 17.
28. Marx, *Capital*, 367.
29. Ibid., 554.
30. Ibid., 554–55.
31. C.f. Marx, *Capital*, 837.
32. Karl Marx, *Manuscripts* (1844), excerpted in *Karl Marx: Early Writings*, ed. Tom Bottomore (New York: McGraw-Hill, 1964), 112–19, and reproduced in Elliott, *Marx and Engels*, 23.
33. Elliott, *Marx and Engels*, 25.
34. See Marty Strange, *Family Farming: A New Economic Vision* (Lincoln: University of Nebraska Press, 1988), ch. 5, "The Myth That Bigger Is Better," 78–103; Kenneth A. Dahlberg, *Beyond the Green Revolution: The Ecology and Politics of Global Agricultural Development* (New York: Plenum Press, 1979), 162; and Anthony Y. C. Koo, *The Role of Land Reform in Economic Development: A Case Study of Taiwan* (New York: Praeger, 1968), 187.
35. Marx, *Capital*, 396.
36. Ibid., 837.
37. Ibid., 697, 836–37; and *Manifesto of the Communist Party* [in Freedman], 24–26.
38. Marx, *Capital*, 536.
39. Mandel, *Marxist Economic Theory*, 13

5. FOR SCIENTIFIC MASTERY OVER LIVING STANDARDS

1. W. Stanley Jevons, *The Theory of Political Economy* [1871], 5th ed. (New York: Kelley & Millman, 1957), xxxiii.
2. Jevons, *Theory*, 44.
3. Ibid., xxxiii.
4. Ibid., 23.
5. Ibid., 37.
6. Ibid., vi, vii.
7. Léon Walras, *Elements of Pure Economics or The Theory of Social Wealth* (1874), trans. William Jaffé (London: George Allen and Unwin, Ltd., 1954), 71.
8. Jevons, *Theory*, 39.
9. Ibid., 168.
10. Ibid., 202–3.
11. Ibid.

12. Ibid., 54.

13. See *Economics in the Future: Towards a New Paradigm*, ed. Kurt Dopfer (Boulder, Colo.: Westview Press, 1976), "Introduction" by Dopfer, 20.

14. Jevons, *Theory*, 45–46.

15. Ibid., 40.

16. Walras, *Elements*, 75.

17. Ibid., 75–77.

18. Alfred Marshall, *Principles of Economics*, 8th ed. (London: MacMillan, 1925), 1.

19. Ibid., 27.

20. Ibid., 28.

21. Jevons, *Theory*, 269–270.

22. Richard G. Lipsey, Peter O. Steiner, Douglas D. Purvis, and Paul N. Courant, *Economics*, 9th ed. (New York: Harper & Row, 1990), 426.

23. Walras, *Elements*, 40.

24. Ibid., 66.

25. See the more thorough discussion of the issue of GNP and the alternative Index of Sustainable Economic Welfare (ISEW) in Daly and Cobb, *For the Common Good*, ch. 3 and Appendix. The ISEW has been further developed and renamed the Genuine Progress Indicator by Clifford Cobb, Ted Halstead, and Jonathan Rowe. See their essay, "If the GDP Is Up, Why Is America Down?" *Atlantic Monthly*, October 1995, 59–78.

26. It would seem that, with respect to nature, we are still mercantilists—*conquistadors* who ransack the natural world for one-time sources of wealth, instead of cultivating ecosystems and harvesting them sustainably. Instead of joining and developing the trading patterns of the new nations they found, the *conquistadors* of the mercantilist period disrupted them for the sake of hauling off all the gold they could find. As a result, Spain and Portugal became wealthy, but only for a short time.

27. See the series of articles on global deforestation (researched for over a year) by A. Kent MacDougall, *Los Angeles Times*, June 14, 17, 19, 22, 1987.

28. Ford Foundation Project on Social Welfare and the American Future, *The Common Good: Social Welfare and the American Future: Policy Recommendations of the Executive Panel* (New York: Ford Foundation, 1989), 16–19.

29. Jevons, *Theory*, 58, 127 ff.

30. Walras, *Elements*, 61.

31. Ibid., 62.

32. Ibid., 63.

33. Ibid., 52.

34. Ibid., 62.

35. Ibid., 216.

36. Ibid., 382.

37. Ibid., 383.
38. Ibid., 388.
39. Marshall, *Principles*, 139.
40. Ibid., 668.
41. Ibid., 169.
42. Ibid., 170.
43. Ibid.
44. Ibid., 139.
45. Ibid., 166.
46. Ibid., 659.
47. Ibid., 193.
48. Ibid., 196–97.
49. Ibid., 654.
50. Ibid., 689.
51. Ibid.
52. Ibid., 690.
53. Ibid., 146.
54. Ibid., 444.
55. Ibid., 777.
56. Ibid., 27.
57. Ibid.
58. Ibid., 57.

6. FOR THE TRIUMPH OF THE ECONOMIC AGENDA OVER HEALTH

1. See, e.g., Richard G. Lipsey, Peter O. Steiner, Douglas D. Purvis, and Paul N. Courant, *Economics*, 9th ed. (New York: Harper & Row, 1990), 363; and Paul A. Samuelson, *Economics*, 11th ed. (New York: McGraw-Hill, 1980), 686.
2. Daniel M. Hausman, ed., *The Philosophy of Economics* (New York: Cambridge University Press, 1984), 35.
3. Peter Drucker, "Toward the Next Economics," *The Crisis in Economic Theory*, ed. Daniel Bell and Irving Kristol (New York: Basic Books, 1981), 8.
4. John Maynard Keynes, *The General Theory of Employment, Interest, and Money* (1935) (New York: Harcourt, Brace & World, 1964), 11.
5. Ibid., 27–28.
6. Ibid., 29.
7. Ibid., 31.
8. Ibid., 31.
9. Ibid., 131.
10. Ibid., 220.

11. Ibid., 46.
12. Ibid., 65.
13. Mark Blaug, *Economic Theory in Retrospect* (Homewood, Ill.: Richard D. Irwin, Inc., 1962), 276.
14. Keynes, *General Theory*, 154–55.
15. Ibid.
16. Ibid., 156.
17. Ibid., 157.
18. Ibid., 159.
19. Ibid.
20. Joseph A. Schumpeter, *Ten Great Economists: From Marx to Keynes* (New York: Oxford University Press, 1951), 282–83.
21. Keynes, *General Theory*, 28.
22. Schumpeter, *Great Economists*, 283, 289.
23. Keynes, *General Theory*, 148.
26. Ibid., 73.
27. Ibid., 213.
28. John Maynard Keynes, *Essays in Persuasion* (New York: W. W. Norton, 1963), 365.
29. Keynes, *General Theory*, 213–14.
30. Blaug, *Economic Theory*, 222
31. Drucker, *The Crisis in Economic Theory*, 10, 9.
32. Charles R. Blaisdell, "Nominalism and Psychoanalysis: A Review Article," *Encounter* 14 (autumn 1986): 372.
33. Milton Friedman, *Capitalism and Freedom* (Chicago: University of Chicago Press, 1962), 5, 6.
34. Ibid., 12.
35. Ibid.
36. Ibid.
37. Ibid..
38. Christopher Hill, *Change and Continuity in 17th Century England* (Cambridge: Harvard University Press, 1975), 236.
39. Friedman, *Capitalism and Freedom*, 13.
40. Ibid., 14.
41. Ibid., 14–15.
42. Ibid., 15.
43. Ibid.
44. See Wes Jackson, *New Roots for Agriculture* (San Francisco: Friends of the Earth, 1980), 31–32, and Kenneth A. Dahlberg, *Beyond the Green Revolution: The Ecology and Politics of Global Agricultural Development* (New York: Plenum Press, 1979), 80–81 and 162–63.

45. Thomas Jefferson, *Notes on the State of Virginia* (1782), in *The Portable Thomas Jefferson*, ed. Merrill D. Peterson (New York: Penguin Books, 1988), 217.

46. Thomas Jefferson, letter to John Adams, October 28, 1813, in *The Portable Thomas Jefferson*, 538.

47. Alexis de Tocqueville describes this contrast in his *Democracy in America* (New York: D. Appleton, 1901), vol. 1, 385–87.

48. Friedman, *Capitalism and Freedom*, 192.

49. Ibid., 30.

50. Milton Friedman, "The Methodology of Positive Economics" (1953), *The Philosophy of Economics*, Daniel M. Hausman, ed., 218.

51. Friedman in Hausman, *The Philosophy of Economics*, 231.

52. Lionel Robbins, *An Essay on the Nature and Significance of Economic Science*, 2d ed. (London: Macmillan, 1935), excerpted in Hausman, *Philosophy of Economics*, 122.

53. Robbins in Hausman, *Philosophy of Economics*, 123.

54. See, e.g., Richard G. Lipsey, Peter O. Steiner, Douglas D. Purvis, and Paul N. Courant, *Economics*, 9th ed. (New York: Harper & Row, 1990), 21, 44; and Campbell R. McConnell and Stanley L. Brue, *Economics: Principles, Problems, and Policies*, 11th ed. (New York: McGraw-Hill, 1990), 39.

55. McConnell and Brue, *Economics*, 21.

56. Kenneth Arrow, *Collected Papers*, vol. 1, *Social Choice and Justice* (Cambridge: Harvard University Press, 1983), 11–12.

CONCLUSION: THE CHOICES FOR HEALTH OVER WEALTH OF NATIONS

1. See Daly and Cobb, *For the Common Good*, Appendix; and Clifford W. Cobb and John B. Cobb Jr., *The Green National Product* (Lanham, Md.: University Press of America, 1994).

2. Mill, *Principles*, 23–25.

3. Absolute scarcity is discussed in chapter 3.

4. Marshall, *Principles*, 139.

5. One of the distinct advantages of using the goal of "health," as opposed to "well-being" or "the common good," is the fact that it is not an anthropocentric concept. It is possible to talk about healthy ecosystems as well as healthy human communities; indeed, it is impossible to have healthy humans without healthy relationships with the rest of the natural world.

6. Intrinsic value is the recognition that all entities have value simply by virtue of existing, apart from any use they may have to human beings or any other entities. Intrinsic value is the philosophical foundation for recognition of the right of other species to exist.

7. See Herman E. Daly and John B. Cobb Jr., *For the Common Good: Economics*

for Community, the Environment, and a Sustainable Future (Boston: Beacon Press, 1989), ch. 8, "From Individualism to Person-in-Community," 159–75.

8. Daly and Cobb, *Common Good,* 161.

9. See, e.g., McConnell and Brue, *Economics,* 45.

10. See Peter F. Drucker, *The New Realities* (New York: Harper & Row, 1989), 210–11.

11. See my booklet, "And the Leaves of the Tree Are for the Healing of the Nations: Biblical and Theological Foundations for Ecojustice" (Louisville: Presbyterian Church USA, 1997).

Bibliography

BOOKS

Arrow, Kenneth. *Collected Papers*. Vol. 1, *Social Choice and Justice*. Cambridge: Harvard University Press, 1983.

Bairoch, Paul. *Cities and Economic Development: From the Dawn of History to the Present*. Chicago: University of Chicago Press, 1988.

Bedau, Hugo A., ed. *Justice and Equality*. Englewood Cliffs, N.J.: Prentice-Hall, 1971.

Bentham, Jeremy. *An Introduction to the Principles of Morals and Legislation*. Edited by J. H. Burns and H. L. A. Hart. London: University of London, Athlone Press, 1970.

————. *The Collected Works of Jeremy Bentham*. Edited by J. R. Dinwiddy. "Deontology" together with "A Table of the Springs of Action" and "The Article on Utilitarianism." Edited by Amnon Goldworth. Oxford: Clarendon Press, 1983.

Berger, Peter L. *The Capitalist Revolution*. New York: Basic Books, 1986.

————. *Pyramids of Sacrifice*. New York: Basic Books, 1974.

Berry, Wendell. *The Unsettling of America: Culture and Agriculture*. San Francisco: Sierra Club Books, 1977.

Blaug, Mark. *Economic Theory in Retrospect*. Homewood, Ill.: Richard D. Irwin, 1962.

Cobb, John B., Jr. *Process Theology as Political Theology*. Philadelphia: Westminster Press, 1982.

Dahlberg, Kenneth A. *Beyond the Green Revolution: The Ecology and Politics of Global Agricultural Development*. New York: Plenum Press, 1979.

Daly, Herman E., and John B. Cobb Jr. *For the Common Good: Redirecting the Economy Toward Community, the Environment, and a Sustainable Future*. Boston: Beacon Press, 1989.

Dopfer, Kurt, ed. *Economics in the Future: Towards a New Paradigm*. Boulder, Colo.: Westview Press, 1976.

Drucker, Peter F. *The New Realities*. New York: Harper & Row, 1989.

Elliott, John E., ed. *Marx and Engels on Economics, Politics, and Society: Essential*

Readings with Editorial Commentary. Santa Monica, Calif.: Goodyear Publishing, 1981.

Ferguson, William. *The Edinburgh History of Scotland.* Vol. 4, *Scotland: 1689 to the Present.* Edinburgh: Mercat Press, 1987.

Ford Foundation Project on Social Welfare and the American Future. *The Common Good: Social Welfare and the American Future: Policy Recommendations of the Executive Panel.* New York: Ford Foundation, 1989.

Fox-Genovese, Elizabeth. *The Origins of Physiocracy: Economic Revolution and Social Order in Eighteenth-Century France.* Ithaca, N.Y.: Cornell University Press, 1976.

Freedman, Robert, ed. *Marx on Economics.* New York: Harcourt, Brace & World, 1961.

Friedman, Milton. *Capitalism and Freedom.* Chicago: University of Chicago Press, 1962.

Galbraith, John Kenneth. *Economics in Perspective: A Critical History.* Boston: Houghton Mifflin, 1987.

Goldschmidt, Walter. *As You Sow: Three Studies in the Social Consequences of Agribusiness.* Montclair, N.J.: Allanheld, Osmun, 1947.

Hausman, Daniel M., ed. *The Philosophy of Economics: An Anthology.* Cambridge: Cambridge University Press, 1984.

Hicks, J. R. *Value and Capital: An Inquiry into Some Fundamental Principles of Economic Theory* (1939). 2d ed. Oxford: Clarendon Press, 1946.

Higgs, Henry. *The Physiocrats: Six Lectures on the French Economistes of the Eighteenth Century.* New York: Langland Press, 1952.

Hill, Christopher. *Change and Continuity in Seventeenth-Century England.* Cambridge: Harvard University Press, 1975.

Hollander, Jacob, ed. *Sir Edward West on the Application of Capital to Land: A Reprint of Economic Tracts* (1815). Baltimore: Johns Hopkins Press, 1903.

Hutcheson, Francis. *Illustrations on the Moral Sense.* Edited by Bernard Peach. Cambridge: Harvard University Press, 1971.

Jackson, Wes. *New Roots for Agriculture.* San Francisco: Friends of the Earth, 1980.

Jevons, W. Stanley. *The Theory of Political Economy* (1871). 5th ed. New York: Kelley & Millman, 1957.

Keynes, John Maynard. *Essays in Persuasion.* New York: W. W. Norton, 1963.

———. *The General Theory of Employment, Interest, and Money* (1935). New York: Harcourt, Brace & World, 1964.

Koo, Anthony Y. C. *The Role of Land Reform in Economic Development: A Case Study of Taiwan.* New York: Praeger, 1968.

Lewis, John P., and Valeriana Kallab, eds. *Development Strategies Reconsidered.* New Brunswick, N.J.: Transaction Books, 1986.

Lipsey, Richard G., Peter O. Steiner, Douglas D. Purvis, and Paul N. Courant. *Economics*. 9th ed. New York: Harper & Row, 1990.

Locke, John. *Two Treatises of Civil Government*. London: J. M. Dent & Sons, 1924.

Malthus, Thomas. *Principles of Political Economy* (1836). Clifton, N.J.: Augustus M. Kelley, 1974.

Mandel, Ernest. *An Introduction to Marxist Economic Theory*. New York: Pathfinder Press, 1970.

Marshall, Alfred. *Principles of Economics*. 8th ed. London: Macmillan, 1925.

Marx, Karl. *Capital*. Edited by Frederick Engels and translation of 3d German edition by Samuel Moore and Edward Aveling. New York: The Modern Library, 1906.

McConnell, Campbell R., and Stanley L. Brue. *Economics: Principles, Problems, and Policies*, 11th ed. New York: McGraw-Hill, 1990.

Meek, Ronald L., ed. *The Economics of Physiocracy: Essays and Translations*. Cambridge: Harvard University Press, 1963.

———. *Marx and Engels on Malthus*. Trans. Dorothea L. Meek and Ronald L. Meek. New York: International Publishers, 1954.

Mill, John Stuart. *On Liberty*. Boston: Ticknor and Fields, 1863.

———. *Principles of Political Economy* (1848). Edited by William Ashley. Clifton, N.J.: Augustus M. Kelley, 1973.

Monroe, Arthur E. *Early Economic Thought*. Cambridge: Harvard University Press, 1924.

Munday, Stephen C. R. *Current Developments in Economics*. New York: St. Martin's Press, 1996.

Novak, Michael. *The Spirit of Democratic Capitalism*. New York: Simon & Schuster, 1982.

Parman, Susan. *Scottish Crofters*. Fort Worth: Holt, Rinehart & Winston, 1990.

Peterson, Merrill D., ed. *The Portable Thomas Jefferson*. New York: Penguin Books, 1988.

Ricardo, David. *The Principles of Political Economy and Taxation* (1817). London: Dent, 1965.

Rima, Ingrid Hahne. *Development of Economic Analysis*. Homewood, Ill.: Richard D. Irwin, 1978.

Robinson, Joan. *Economic Heresies: Some Old-Fashioned Questions in Economic Theory*. New York: Basic Books, 1971.

———. *Economic Philosophy*. Harmondsworth, Middlesex, England: Penguin Books, 1962.

———. *What Are the Questions?* Armonk, N.Y.: M. E. Sharpe, 1980.

Samuelson, Paul A. *Economics*. 11th ed. New York: McGraw-Hill, 1980.

Schumpeter, Joseph A. *The History of Economic Analysis* (1954). Edited by Elizabeth Boody Schumpeter. New York: Oxford University Press, 1986.

———. *Ten Great Economists: From Marx to Keynes.* New York: Oxford University Press, 1951.

Smith, Adam. *An Inquiry into the Nature and Causes of the Wealth of Nations* (1776). Edited by Edwin Cannan. New York: Modern Library, 1937.

———. *The Theory of Moral Sentiments.* London: Henry G. Bohm, 1853.

Smout, T. C. *A Century of the Scottish People: 1830–1950.* New Haven, Conn.: Yale University Press, 1986.

Stigler, George. *Essays in the History of Economics.* Chicago: University of Chicago Press, 1965.

Strange, Marty. *Family Farming: A New Economic Vision.* Lincoln: University of Nebraska Press, 1988.

Taylor, John B. *Economics.* Boston: Houghton Mifflin, 1995.

Tinbergen, Jan. *Jan Tinbergen: Selected Papers.* Edited by L. H. Klaassen, L. M. Koyck, and H. J. Witteveen. Amsterdam: North Holland, 1959.

Tocqueville, Alexis de. *Democracy in America.* New York: D. Appleton, 1901.

Viner, Jacob. *The Long View and the Short: Studies in Economic Theory and Policy.* Glencoe, Ill.: The Free Press, 1958.

———. *The Role of Providence in the Social Order.* Philadelphia: American Philosophical Society, 1972.

Walras, Léon. *Elements of Pure Economics or The Theory of Social Wealth* (1874). Trans. William Jaffé. London: George Allen and Unwin, 1954.

Witherspoon, John. *An Annotated Edition of "Lectures on Moral Philosophy."* Edited by Jack Scott. Newark: University of Delaware Press, 1982.

ESSAYS, EXCERPTS, AND ARTICLES

Blaisdell, Charles R. "Nominalism and Psychoanalysis: A Review Article." *Encounter* 47 (autumn 1986): 371–77.

Blaug, Mark. "Was There a Marginal Revolution?" *History of Political Economy* 4 (1972): 269–80.

Brems, Hans. "Cantillon versus Marx: The Land Theory and the Labor Theory of Value." *History of Political Economy* 10 (winter 1978): 669–78.

de Mirabeau, the Marquise. *Correspondance Générale de J. J. Rousseau.* Edited by T. Dufour, vol. 17 (1932). In *The Economics of Physiocracy: Essays and Translations,* edited by Ronald L. Meek. Cambridge: Harvard University Press, 1963.

Drucker, Peter. "Toward the Next Economics." In *The Crisis in Economic Theory,* edited by Daniel Bell and Irving Kristol. New York: Basic Books, 1981.

Friedman, Milton. "The Methodology of Positive Economics" (1953). In *The Philosophy of Economics: An Anthology,* edited by Daniel M. Hausman. Cambridge: Cambridge University Press, 1984.

Gilbert, Geoffrey. "Economic Growth and the Poor in Malthus' Essay on Population." *History of Political Economy* 12 (spring 1980): 83–96.

Harris, Marvin. "Murders in Eden." In *Anthropology: Contemporary Perspectives*, edited by David E. K. Hunter and Phillip Whitten. Boston: Little, Brown, 1985.

Jefferson, Thomas. *Notes on the State of Virginia* (1782). In *The Portable Thomas Jefferson*, edited by Merrill D. Peterson. New York: Penguin Books, 1988.

Johnston, Carol. "And the Leaves of the Tree Are for the Healing of the Nations: Biblical and Theological Foundations for Ecojustice." Louisville: Presbyterian Church USA, 1997.

Keynes, John Neville. "The Scope and Method of Political Economy" (1917). Reprinted in *The Philosophy of Economics: An Anthology*, edited by Daniel M. Hausman. Cambridge: Cambridge University Press, 1984.

Krueger, Alan B. "The Truth about Wages." *New York Times*, July 31, 1997.

MacDougall, A. Kent. Series: "The Vanishing Forests." *Los Angeles Times*, June 14, 17, 19, 22, 1987.

Marx, Karl. *Grundrisse: Foundations of the Critique of Political Economy*. Trans. Martin Nicolaus. New York: Random House, 1973. In *The Philosophy of Economics*, edited by Daniel M. Hausman. Cambridge: Cambridge University Press, 1984.

———. Manuscripts (1844). Excerpted in *Karl Marx: Early Writings*, edited by Tom Bottomore. New York: McGraw-Hill, 1964. Reproduced in *Marx and Engels on Economics, Politics, and Society: Essential Readings with Editorial Commentary*, edited by John E. Elliott. Santa Monica, Calif.: Goodyear Publishing, 1981.

———. *Theories of Surplus Value* (1861–63], English edition 1952. In *Marx and Engels on Malthus*, edited by Ronald L. Meek. Translated by Dorothea L. Meek and Ronald L. Meek. New York: International Publishers, 1954.

Marx, Karl, and Friedrich Engels. *The German Ideology* (1845–46), excerpts from Part 1. In *Marx and Engels on Economics, Politics, and Society: Essential Readings with Editorial Commentary*, edited by John E. Elliott. Santa Monica, Calif.: Goodyear Publishing, 1981.

———. *Manifesto of the Communist Party* (1848). Edited by Friedrich Engels and translated by Samuel Moore. New York: International Publishers, 1932. Reprinted in *Marx on Economics*, edited by Robert Freedman. New York: Harcourt, Brace & World, 1961.

Mathias, Peter. "Agriculture and Industrialization." In *The First Industrial Revolutions*, edited by Peter Mathias and John A. Davis. Oxford: Basil Blackwell, 1989.

Mill, John Stuart. "On the Definition and Method of Political Economy." In *The Philosophy of Economics*, edited by Daniel M. Hausman. Cambridge: Cambridge University Press, 1984.

Quesnay, François. "Corn," translated from the text as reproduced in François

Quesnay et la Physiocratie. Paris: Institut National d'Etudes Démographiques, 1958. In *The Economics of Physiocracy*, edited by Ronald L. Meek. Cambridge: Harvard University Press, 1963.

Winch, Donald. "Marginalism and the Boundaries of Economic Science." *History of Political Economy* 4 (1972): 325–43.

Index

absolute natural abundance, 41
absolute scarcity, 38–41, 52, 61
agribusiness, 54–55
agriculture, 13–17, 38, 52–55; industrialization of, 72–74; in Switzerland, 52–53. *See also* land
Arrow, Kenneth, 108
assumptions, 106–8, 121–22
authority, centralized, 26–28

Berger, Peter, 2, 17, 19–20, 66
Blaisdell, Charles, 101
Blaug, Mark, 96, 100

Calvin, John, 7
capital: land as, 87–88, 99–100, 125–26; money as, 55–56; role of, 44
Capital (Marx), 67, 73
capitalism: costs of, 1–3, 19; development of, 1–2; goal of, 76; responses to problems of, 2–4; transformation of, 3–4, 8–9
Capitalist Revolution, The (Berger), 17
central authority, 26–28
centralized decision-making, 121
"civilized" versus "savage" nations, 18–21
clear-cutting of forests, 84
Cobb, John B., Jr., 8
collective man, 76
commodities, 67–70, 80
common lands, 36, 74–75, 102
communism, 3
comparative advantage theory, 31–33
competition, 26–28
conservatives, 58
consumerism, 2
consumption, 80, 95–96
Corn Laws, 18, 29, 34, 35–38, 65
credit, 94
cultural marginalism, 85

Daly, Herman, 114
decision-making, centralized, 121
deductive method, 7, 30–34, 46, 47–48, 50, 55, 121–22
demand, effective, 95
demand and supply, 35–36, 37, 56–57, 62, 77, 94
democracy, 53–54
diminishing returns, law of, 16, 35–36, 51–52, 77–78, 87

distribution, 34–35, 46–47, 57–58, 93; production and distribution of wealth, 56–57; redistribution, 47, 57–58, 93
disutility, 86
diversity, 123, 126
division of labor, 19
doctrine of God, 128–30
Drucker, Peter, xiv, 94, 100–101

economic growth, 11–23, 45, 62–63; endless growth, 59–60; as goal of the economy, 80; and industrialization, 67; and rights of individuals, 66; in 20th-century economics, 92; and wealth maximizing, 47–50
economic method, 79–80
economics: and desire for wealth, 47–50; development of, 6–8; environmental economics, 5; goal of, 90–91, 119–21; macroeconomics, 90, 96; neoclassical economics, 4–6, 77, 107; as a science, 30–31, 77, 79, 81, 86, 90–91; transforming, 119–26; in 20th century, 92–93, 118–19; value choices in development of, 6–7
economic theory, 79–80, 121–22
economists, learning from, 112–19
economy, goal of, 80, 88
effective demand, principle of, 95
embodied labor, 67, 70, 72
employment/unemployment, 94–96
endless growth, 59–60
environmental economics, 5
environmental regulations, 32
Essay on the Principle of Population, An (Malthus), 44
exchange value, 36, 37–41, 44, 61–62, 68–69; as creation of labor, 70; and embodied labor, 70; and interaction of scarcity and utility, 78; labor as measure of, 67–70; and nature, 69–70; versus exchange value, 67–69. *See also* labor theory of value
export-driven development, 16–17
exports, 14–17
externalities, 82–83

factory farming, 54–55
factory labor, 21–22, 36
factory system, 75–76

Made in the USA
Las Vegas, NV
15 January 2021

15977980R10095